OVERDUE NOTICES A
OF THE LIBRARY. BO
OBLIGATED TO RET
ON TIME WITHOUT

Identity Theft
in the 21st Century

CRIME SCENE INVESTIGATIONS

By Sarah Machajewski

Portions of this book originally appeared in
Identity Theft by Gail B. Stewart.

LUCENT PRESS

Published in 2018 by
Lucent Press, an Imprint of Greenhaven Publishing, LLC
353 3rd Avenue
Suite 255
New York, NY 10010

Copyright © 2018 Greenhaven Press, a part of Gale, Cengage Learning
Gale and Greenhaven Press are registered trademarks used herein under license.

All new materials copyright © 2018 Lucent Press, an Imprint of Greenhaven Publishing, LLC.

All rights reserved. No part of this book may be reproduced in any form without permission in writing from the publisher, except by a reviewer.

Designer: Deanna Paternostro
Editor: Siyavush Saidian

Library of Congress Cataloging-in-Publication Data

Names: Machajewski, Sarah.
Title: Identity theft in the 21st century / Sarah Machajewski.
Description: New York : Lucent Press, 2018. | Series: Crime scene investigations | Includes index.
Identifiers: ISBN 9781534560833 (library bound) | ISBN 9781534560840 (ebook)
Subjects: LCSH: Identity theft–United States–Juvenile literature. | Online identity theft–Juvenile literature.
Classification: LCC HV6679.M33 2018 | DDC 364.16'330973–dc23

Printed in the United States of America

CPSIA compliance information: Batch #BS17KL: For further information contact Greenhaven Publishing LLC, New York, New York at 1-844-317-7404.

Please visit our website, www.greenhavenpublishing.com. For a free color catalog of all our high-quality books, call toll free 1-844-317-7404 or fax 1-844-317-7405.

Contents

Foreword	4
Introduction:	
An Invisible Crime	6
Chapter One:	
Bad Business at the Bank	16
Chapter Two:	
Identity Theft in the Mailbox	32
Chapter Three:	
A Closeup Look at Credit Card Fraud	44
Chapter Four:	
Posing as Someone Else	57
Chapter Five:	
Computers, Cybercrime, and Identity Theft	70
Chapter Six:	
Staying Safe	88
Notes	92
For More Information	96
Index	98
Picture Credits	103
About the Author	104

Foreword

For decades, popular television programs and movies have depicted the life and work of police officers, detectives, and crime scene investigators. Most of these shows and films portray forensic scientists as the brains responsible for cracking cases and bringing criminals to justice. Undoubtedly, these crime scene analysts are an important part in the process of crime solving. With modern technology and advances in forensic analysis, these highly trained experts are a crucial component of law enforcement systems all across the world.

Police officers and detectives are also integral members of the law enforcement team. They are the ones who respond to 911 calls about crime, collect physical evidence, and use their high level of training to identify suspects and culprits. They work right alongside forensic investigators to figure out the mysteries behind why a crime is committed, and the entire team cooperates to gather enough evidence to convict someone in a court of law.

Ever since the first laws were recorded, crime scene investigation has been handled in roughly the same way. An authority is informed that a crime has been committed; someone looks around the crime scene and interviews potential witnesses; suspects are identified based on evidence and testimony; and, finally, someone is formally accused of committing a crime. This basic plan is generally effective, and criminals are often caught and brought to justice. Throughout history, however, certain limitations have sometimes prevented authorities from finding out who was responsible for a crime.

There are many reasons why a crime goes unsolved: Maybe a dead body was found too late, evidence was tampered with, or witnesses lied. Sometimes, even the greatest technology of the age is simply not good enough to process and analyze the evidence at a crime scene. In the United States during the 20th century, for example, the person responsible for the infamous Zodiac killings was never found, despite the earnest efforts of hundreds of policemen, detectives, and forensic analysts.

In modern times, science and technology are integral to the investigative process. From DNA analysis to high-definition surveillance video, it has become much more difficult to commit a crime and get away with it. Using advanced computers and immense databases, microscopic skin cells from a crime scene can be collected and then analyzed by a forensic scientist, leading detectives to the home of the culprit of a crime. Dozens of people work behind the scenes of criminal investigations to figure out the unique and complex elements of a crime. Although this process is still time-consuming and complicated, technology is constantly improving and adapting to the needs of police forces worldwide.

This series is designed to help young readers understand the systems in place to allow forensic professionals to do their jobs. Covering a wide range of topics, from the assassination of President John F. Kennedy to 21st-century cybercriminals, these titles describe in detail the ways in which technology and criminal investigations have evolved over more than 50 years. They cite eyewitnesses and experts in order to give a detailed and nuanced picture of the difficult task of rooting out criminals. Although television shows and movies add drama to the crime scene investigation process, these real-life stories have enough drama on their own. This series sticks to the facts surrounding some of the highest-profile criminal cases of the modern era and the people who work to solve them and other crimes every day.

Introduction
An Invisible Crime

Brendan Peterson set out on a cold December day with big plans in mind. He was headed to a jewelry store in downtown Chicago and he was very excited. "I was going to buy a ring," he said. "I was going to propose to my girlfriend, Mara, on Christmas Eve, so I was running over to the store during my lunch hour. She didn't know I was proposing that soon—it was going to be a big surprise."[1]

The jewelry store had a ring Brendan knew Mara would love. When it came time to pay, he decided to use his credit card. He handed the salesperson his credit card, and when the salesperson walked away, Brendan began thinking of how he was going to propose. His daydreaming was quickly brought to a halt. When the salesperson came back, she told Brendan there was a problem—his credit card had been declined.

Brendan was surprised to hear this, thinking the salesperson may have somehow entered the credit card number incorrectly. It must have been a simple mistake. "I called the customer service number [of the credit card company] from the store," he said. "I was told that I had several other [Visa] cards—even the one I only use for business—that were maxed out, and that they would not accept a charge from me. It wasn't a mistake."[2]

Understanding Identity Theft

Brendan did not use the credit cards himself—the cashier's news came as a total shock. So what happened? Brendan was a victim of identity theft. Identity theft happens when somebody steals another person's personal information, such as their name, Social Security number, or credit card number, and uses it without their permission. Typically, the information is used for their own personal gain or for

Widespread use of computers and credit cards has changed the way thieves steal sensitive information.

profit. Identity theft is a serious crime, but it is not a new one. Ever since people have been storing their money in banks, identity theft has occurred. People try to claim they are someone they are not, and sometimes, the protective measures banks have in place are not enough.

What is new, however, is the way modern identity thieves are operating in the 21st century. It is no longer as simple as forging a signature or pretending to be someone. With the rise of credit cards across the world, identity thieves can attack someone's life digitally, stealing their credit card number and running up huge bills. Many people use their computers and cell phones to store personal information, and if a criminal gets their

8 Identity Theft in the 21st Century

State and federal law enforcement agencies are involved in the fight against identity theft. Authorities frequently hold press conferences similar to this one, announcing the arrests of identity thieves and explaining their crimes.

hands on these devices, it can lead to identity theft.

According to the Federal Bureau of Investigation (FBI), identity theft is one of the fastest growing crimes in the United States. Independent studies have estimated that more than 15 million people were victims of identity theft in 2016. In a world that is becoming more digital every day, experts only expect that number to increase. Faced with the explosion of new cases in the United States, investigators who once aimed to reduce the rate of identity theft are now focused on just slowing its increase.

Pay Attention or Pay the Price

Identity theft is a serious crime, and so are its consequences. Identity theft can be financially devastating. First, many victims find themselves forced to pay for purchases they never made. Samantha, a teacher from Minneapolis and an identity theft victim, said:

> *I wasn't paying attention to my [credit card] statements every month. I ... kind of just closed my eyes and wrote the check every month for the minimum payment. Anyway, for eight months, somebody was charging stuff on my card. Nothing huge—otherwise I would have spotted it. Just a couple hundred here and there. By the time I really paid attention, [the thief] bought more than $1,500 worth of stuff ... If I'd told the card company earlier, they said they might have been able to do something about it ... But since those purchases were mixed up within my own, they wouldn't do anything. So that's an extra $1,500 I'll never see, I guess.*[3]

Though personal stories similar to this are sad, they are far from uncommon. Thousands of people have their personal information stolen every day, and some face much worse consequences than losing $1,500. Some people have lost their cars, their homes, and even their jobs because of identity theft.

Dealing with the Consequences of Identity Theft

Identity theft victims may find that more than their identity has been taken from them. Thieves frequently rob them of their money—and their time. Some victims manage to get banks or credit card companies to forgive the charges made by the thieves, but this process can be time-consuming. The Federal Trade Commission reports that it takes 18 months, on average, to recover from identity theft. However, even when bank charges are forgiven, some businesses may not reimburse victims for merchandise bought with fake credit cards. Many victims must pay fees to get their credit cards back in good standing, or they have to pay fees associated with writing bad checks. They sometimes need to pay for lawyers during this time, too. Because of such expenses, victims of personal information fraud lose an average of $7,761. Victims of bank fraud lose an average of $780.

Resolving an identity theft situation can feel like putting together pieces of a puzzle. This process is even more difficult for the many victims who are viewed with suspicion by customer service agents and bank officials. "I don't know of many crimes where the victim has to convince people she's the [victim]," said Samantha. "I had to keep telling my story to different people, and they'd switch me to someone else, and I'd have to tell it all over again. I didn't get a lot of sympathy, that's for sure."[4] Many victims of identity theft go through a similar process. They are forced to insist that they are innocent countless times.

Most victims would agree that the process of repairing the damage of identity theft is extremely stressful, with no guarantee of a satisfying resolution. Even if fraudulent charges are forgiven, or banks and credit card companies replace the stolen cash, many victims suffer other damaging financial consequences—especially

Total Fraud Victims Reaches Record High

Millions of U.S. Fraud Victims

Year	Victims (millions)
2011	11.6
2012	12.6
2013	13.1
2014	12.7
2015	13.1
2016	15.4

As this information from Javelin Strategy & Research shows, the number of identity theft victims has been rising, hitting a record high in 2016.

A credit score measures someone's creditworthiness—or how likely they are to pay for their debt. It is an important tool banks use when deciding if they can extend a loan to a customer.

to their credit rating. A credit rating is a measure of a person's financial stability and is largely based on the person's history of paying bills and loans. A falling credit rating can be a sign of identity theft. With a bad credit rating, it is harder to get loans for common needs, such as a car or a home. It is difficult to repair credit.

A person with a low credit rating is considered a high-risk borrower, less likely to get loan approval and more likely to pay higher interest rates—even years after the crime. Identity theft victims suffer twice. Experts agree that identity theft is a terrible crime. The interest rates on loans given to people with bad credit can be more than three or four times as high as people with good credit.

A Crime Unlike Any Other

Identity theft is a terrible crime in part because it is so difficult to solve. Police say it is unlike other crimes in significant ways. As one Minneapolis, Minnesota, police officer remarked, "There is often no crime scene. You can't say, 'This is exactly where it happened, now get the [evidence] guys in here to process it.' You typically don't have ... DNA for ID theft. There's no ballistics evidence, or anything like that."[5]

Another difference between identity theft and other crimes is that most victims cannot even say for sure when the crime occurred. In fact, about 45 percent of identity theft victims first learn about the crime when a financial institution, such as their bank, contacts them about suspicious activity.

One man whose credit cards were used to run up charges of more than $30,000 claimed that he did not understand how his identity could have been stolen:

> My credit cards never were taken. Nobody picked my pocket or broke into my house. But the numbers were used to buy a lot of stuff. The police officer I talked to told me it could have been ID theft rings that used computers, originating anywhere from Nigeria to Thailand. How do they investigate something like that, when it doesn't even happen [in the United States]?[6]

Sometimes, a single case of identity theft involves dozens or hundreds of similarly unidentifiable "crime scenes," linked in incredibly complex ways. Jessica and her husband found this out the hard way. When they applied to refinance their Wisconsin home, the bank turned down their application. The couple was told that a number of their credit card and loan payments were past due.

Since they knew nothing of these accounts, it was clear that they were victimized by an identity thief. An investigation found that a woman in Texas had applied for credit 19 times using Jessica's name and Social Security number. In all, the thief had racked up more than $60,000 in purchases, from cell phones to a mobile home to a new car, all in Jessica's name. Each credit card and loan was issued by a different bank. Because of the number of banks and stores involved, the theft of Jessica's personal information had resulted in 19 different crimes. "When a good thief gets busy," noted one identity theft expert, "he gets really busy."[7]

An Invisible Crime **13**

These cards were seized by police in a large identity theft bust. Experienced criminals will often carry hundreds of fraudulent cards.

Low Priority to Law Enforcement

The job of untangling intricate webs of identity theft is difficult because law enforcement resources are limited. Identity thieves are skilled at using complex technologies to commit their crimes, and few police departments have the money to hire enough people with highly technical computer expertise. Additionally, law enforcement agencies may not see the value in assigning officers to investigate what are primarily known as crimes against property. Solving violent crimes, such as murder, rape, and assault—known as crimes against persons—takes priority.

Sometimes, federal agencies such as the FBI get involved in identity theft cases. However, given the sheer number of identity theft cases reported every year, even federal resources

An FBI official is shown here detailing how the evidence of a big case came together.

must target the highest-priority cases. Because large companies deal with large sums of money, identity thieves can get away with a lot more. If one company had $50,000 stolen and another had $1 million stolen, the FBI will investigate the case that caused the most loss. This can be devastating to a company of any size, and there is simply not a lot that can be done about it.

Despite the lack of investigative resources and the rising number of reported crimes, many cases of identity theft do get solved. Most of those cases do not hinge on scientific breakthroughs in the crime lab. Instead, as the number of identity thefts involving computers grows, detectives must develop new investigative techniques and follow new kinds of evidence trails. Increasingly, they rely on the latest electronic security software and diagnostic tools.

"You've got to remember that the bad guys have a lot of the same tools," said one Minneapolis investigator:

And just when we think we're getting a little bit ahead of the game, they come up with a new way to grab sensitive information they have absolutely no business having. ID theft is a constant war against a criminal we may never see face-to-face—we will probably not catch most of them. But in many ways, it's a huge victory if we can just prevent them from ruining people's lives.[8]

Chapter One
Bad Business at the Bank

There are many forms of identity theft, but what they all have in common is that the thief is using someone else's information for financial gain. Identity thieves typically want to pay for things with someone else's money. Where better to find money than at the bank?

Check fraud is a kind of identity theft that does not involve high-tech skills. Checks contain two important pieces of information: a person's name and their bank account number. The person whose name is on the check is the owner of the funds in the bank account. They are responsible for supplying the money when a check from their account is cashed.

When somebody pays with a check, it is assumed they are actually the person whose name is on it. Bankers and retail employees are trained to check ID when a customer pays with a check. However, this is far from a foolproof way to prevent crime. As the 21st century progresses, fewer people use checks to pay for household items. As a result, check fraud is not as common as it was in the 20th century. However, most people still have checkbooks, and if they fall into the wrong hands, their rightful owners can find themselves the victims of identity theft.

Taking Total Advantage

Unlike cyber identity theft, check fraud can typically only occur if a thief has a physical copy of someone's checkbook. As a result, someone who steals checks may have instant access to someone's bank account. Because most people frequently pay with cash or cards, they may not immediately notice that a thief is using their checks. This can be incredibly damaging to their bank account, their credit, and their life.

The sooner a victim of check fraud calls their bank, the better. Bank

A check gives someone access to the money in a specific bank account. Because most checks do not have digital security protection, it is important to keep checkbooks safe.

officials can freeze, or stop, any transactions to or from an account. This can help ensure that no new checks can be processed until the matter is settled. This is the best way that a person can protect their funds because the checks will essentially become worthless. The longer it takes to notice a missing checkbook, however, the more damage can be done. Over the course of a single day, a criminal could make thousands of dollars' worth of unauthorized purchases. If that happens, there is only so much help the bank can offer.

One or Two Is All It Takes

Fraudulent, or "bad," checks are written and processed every business day in the United States and other countries. Some cases involve the theft of an entire checkbook. In many cases, however, claimed one Minneapolis police officer, a thief steals just one or two checks from a victim's checkbook. "That's smart, if you're a thief," he said:

It makes it harder for the victim to notice right away. Most people don't write the check and amount [down] when they write the check. So if a check or two are gone, chances are the victim just figures he or she didn't record the amount. So instead of calling the bank and [freezing] their account, the victim just thinks, "Okay, where did I write check number 3535? Was it at the grocery store or for my kid's hot lunch program at school?" They just assume they forgot to write it down. And it isn't until the end of the month, when the bank statement comes, that they realize what happened.[9]

This officer claimed that this type of identity thief is generally careful to keep the amount of the check low enough not to be questioned. "They usually keep a purchase to $100 or less," he said. "A thief knows he'd better write a check or two quick, before the victim finds out [checks] are missing, and tells the bank to freeze the account. It's a race."[10]

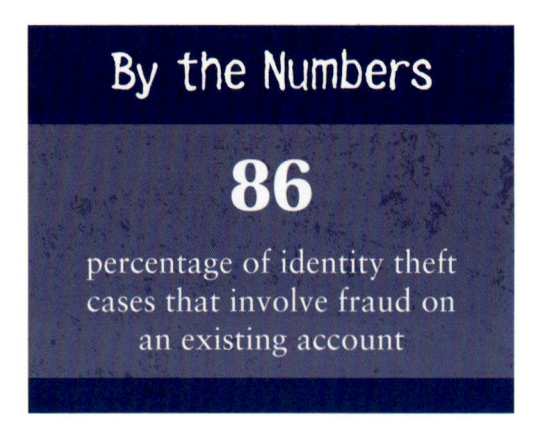

By the Numbers

86

percentage of identity theft cases that involve fraud on an existing account

Speaking Up When Something Is Wrong

Investigators claim the success or failure of check fraud is often dependent on a retail employee's actions. Many stores routinely require a second form of identification, such as a driver's license with the owner's photograph, when a customer pays by check. The chance that the check is stolen is low if the information on the check and additional ID matches, and the photograph actually shows the person who is writing the check. This basic level of protection helps save potential identity theft victims every single day.

All it takes is one inattentive clerk or low-security store to cause a victim serious financial ruin. Sometimes,

Today, millions of people use smartphones to handle their banking—including depositing checks into their bank accounts. Without any face-to-face interaction, however, it can be hard to spot fraud when it happens.

even when a thief presents their own driver's license with a stolen check, many clerks fail to notice that the name on the check and the name on the license do not match. If they noticed, they could decline the sale and protect the victim.

"This is really disturbing, but it happens every day," claimed one manager of a large grocery store:

Clerks are overworked and busy. They've got lines of people waiting to check out, and they often just do

Different handwriting is a fairly obvious sign of a fraudulent check.

a quick look at the picture—and how many people look like the picture on their driver's license anyway? Though they are trained to compare the address on the check to that on the license, many don't. A lot of the time, the clerk is more interested in making sure the check amount is right. So the [criminal] gets through without a hitch.[11]

An alert clerk who spots something wrong can make all the difference. Confronting a thief, or simply refusing to make a sale to a suspicious customer, will not only protect the victim, but it can also help put the criminal behind bars. There are countless stories of cashiers who called their store's security team to deal with a customer who looked like

Almost Uncatchable

One of history's most notorious identity thieves is Frank Abagnale Jr. Born in 1948, Abagnale began his career in crime by shoplifting when he was a teenager. After leaving home at age 16, he spent the next five years cashing bad checks, scamming companies out of money, and convincing hundreds of people that he was an airline pilot, a doctor, or an attorney. Authorities finally caught up to Abagnale in 1969 when he was arrested in France after being turned in by a former girlfriend. After serving five years in prison, he went on to become a prominent security adviser, helping banks and governments fight against other identity thieves. He was able to get away with his crimes for years because of the relatively unsophisticated technology of the 1960s. In the modern world, with computer databases, highly trained officials, and fraud protection protocols, it would be impossible to convincingly lie to so many people for so long. A partially fictional movie about Abagnale's life, titled *Catch Me If You Can*, was released in 2002.

they were trying to use a check that did not belong to them.

Minneapolis police lieutenant Steve Kincaid says this is exactly how check-writing safeguards are supposed to work:

> The store security will try to hold them until [police] can respond. Hopefully, we can get the cavalry ... there in time to grab them. Sometimes, a clerk will stall them by saying that the computers are down, and the customer should come back in half an hour to pick up the items he purchased. You'd be surprised—some of these guys are dumb enough to come back.[12]

Investigative Experience Is Essential

Not every identity thief is caught in the act of paying for something with a fraudulent check. Sometimes they are caught after the fact, thanks to law enforcement's investigative procedures. Investigators are able to narrow down a list of suspects based on their experience investigating other cases of identity theft. They know, for example, that in many cases of check identity theft, the thief is someone the victim knows—a coworker or even a family member.

Bank investigators see countless cases in which a teen or child of the victim is responsible for the identity theft. "It may be an older child with a drug or gambling problem. In instances like these, a victim often suspects that might be the case and may be unwilling for us to pursue the investigation."[13]

In other cases, a victim's specific circumstances may provide clues to a thief's identity. For example, disabled or elderly people often rely on others for help. "They might depend on a home health worker to come in, or a neighbor to get groceries or pick up medication from the drug store," said a Minnesota woman who works with disabled and elderly adults. "And instead of doing their work honestly, they take advantage."[14]

Chemically Altered to Commit Fraud

Simply signing a victim's name to a check is one type of check fraud. It is not the only way to do it, however. In fact, there are two other methods that are both more complicated and more profitable for thieves.

Washing checks is another form of check identity theft. A "washed" check is one that has been honestly filled out and signed by its owner, then stolen and chemically altered by a thief. The thief uses a chemical solution that can take ink off the paper. Their goal is to make the check look as if it is payable to them. Check washing used to be a common form of check fraud. Experts have reported that upward of $815 million worth of washed checks are passed each year in the United States.

Though less frequent in the 21st century, check washing is still something consumers have to protect themselves against. If someone is careless, thieves can easily get their hands on other people's checks. The most common method is to steal personal mail that is likely to contain a payment by check, such as mail addressed to a credit card or utility company. The stolen checks are taken to a makeshift workshop, where thieves use a range of common chemicals to erase the ink on the checks. Because such chemicals are sold at many drug or grocery stores, their purchase would not raise any red flags with store personnel.

Typically, the name on the check's "pay to the order of" line is changed—either to the thief's real name or to a name for which they have a fake identification. In many cases, the dollar amount is increased, too. Thieves are careful to leave the signature intact, however. Any changes they make to the check are written in the same handwriting and ink color as the signature. Although using a single ink color everywhere on a check is not a requirement for a legitimate check, multiple colors of ink can raise suspicion in an alert employee where the stolen check is eventually deposited or cashed.

While check washing is something consumers must still be aware of, the increasing use of online bill payment technology is helping to combat the problem. Online bill payment systems provide a safe, secure way for people to pay their bills without having to put a check in the mail—or compromise their bank accounts.

By the Numbers

15

percentage of people who will experience identity theft in their lifetime

Check Fraud by Way of Computer

The third and most technologically advanced form of check identity theft is accomplished not by chemical alteration, but with a computer, scanner, and printer. By printing fake checks with real account numbers, thieves can create business or personal checks that often look completely legitimate to most people.

One bank fraud investigator claimed this kind of identity theft begins with software programs sold in most office-supply stores that enable businesses to print their own checks:

There's no law that says people have to buy checks from the bank, or from those companies that advertise in the coupon section of the newspaper. You can buy check paper stock that looks exactly like the paper bank checks are printed on, too. The technology is out there—it's just that crooks have found a way to use it for illegal purposes.[15]

These identity thieves, like those who wash checks, rely on real account numbers. Police investigators point out that these numbers can be obtained in a variety of ways. "Sometimes it's stolen mail, like other types of ID theft. They don't use the check, just the information on it, when they make their own. They also get numbers from hanging around the bank, keeping an eye on people making transactions there."[16]

Many identity thieves use a tactic called "shoulder-surfing," or casually standing behind a customer. They do this so they can be close enough to read an account number or a deposit amount. Another method is simply retrieving a discarded receipt from the bank after a deposit or withdrawal is made.

Lower Risk, Higher Success

By printing their own checks, criminals can easily avoid many of the risks encountered by check washers or those who simply forge the victim's signature on a check. For one thing, they make sure they have a fake identification, such as a fake driver's license, for whatever name they use on the check. In fact, some identity thieves have been known to possess more than a thousand different IDs. This allows them to avoid using the same name more than a few times.

For the same reason, criminals will not use the same account number for more than a check or two. They are smart enough to realize that with a few strokes on their computer keyboard, they can simply create a new

Counterfeit checks are made to look identical to real checks, such as this one. This makes some identity thieves very difficult to track and catch.

check with a new account number and new name. Additionally, they avoid suspicion by writing checks for only moderately small amounts. It is rare for a cashier or teller to see if a name and account number match. Typically, they only make sure the name matches the driver's license or other identification. Only when the check is processed—after it is cashed—would an issue be found. By that time, the identity thief is on to another account number and will be difficult to find.

In 2014, an identity theft organization in Minnesota was caught producing about 1,500 counterfeit, or fake, checks. Law enforcement officials determined the organization attempted to steal $2 million from banks in Minnesota and several other states. Called the largest and most sophisticated identity theft organization in Minnesota, the criminals were able to operate from 2007 to 2014 and victimized everyone from dentists to teenagers who had posted pictures of their paychecks on social media. Law enforcement officials took down the organization by using surveillance video and GPS devices to track criminals' comings and goings. The situation was a reminder that everyone must always be careful with personal information and never post such personal information online.

By the Numbers

15

years that identity theft has been the number-one consumer complaint to the Federal Trade Commission

Catching the Bad Guys

Check fraud is a serious crime. Luckily, investigators are able to catch many of the bad guys. One Minneapolis police officer said:

These guys aren't superheroes. Many of them trip up, and they are arrested. One of the most common ways they're caught is at the point where they're cashing the check. We'll get a bank teller or a cashier at a store who spots a forgery or a washed check, and that helps us out a lot.[17]

Bank tellers and cashiers are commonly trained to examine a check and ID carefully before accepting it as payment. Many times, it is in the fine details of a check that the identity thief slips up. For example, in creating a check, the thief may not be careful about the spelling of words in the

Law enforcement agents across the globe are always on the lookout for fraudulent checks so they can protect potential victims.

address. "Misspellings are big," said another officer. "We get a lot of counterfeit checks with misspelled states, streets—even cities."[18]

Careless Mistakes

Identity thieves can also give themselves away by making careless mistakes in the numbers on the checks they forge. At the bottom of every check, for example, is a sequence of numbers that mean something specific. The checking account number is part of it. The number also contains the number of the Federal Reserve District where the bank is located. The United States is divided into 12 official banking districts, and each is assigned a unique number.

For example, if the bank whose

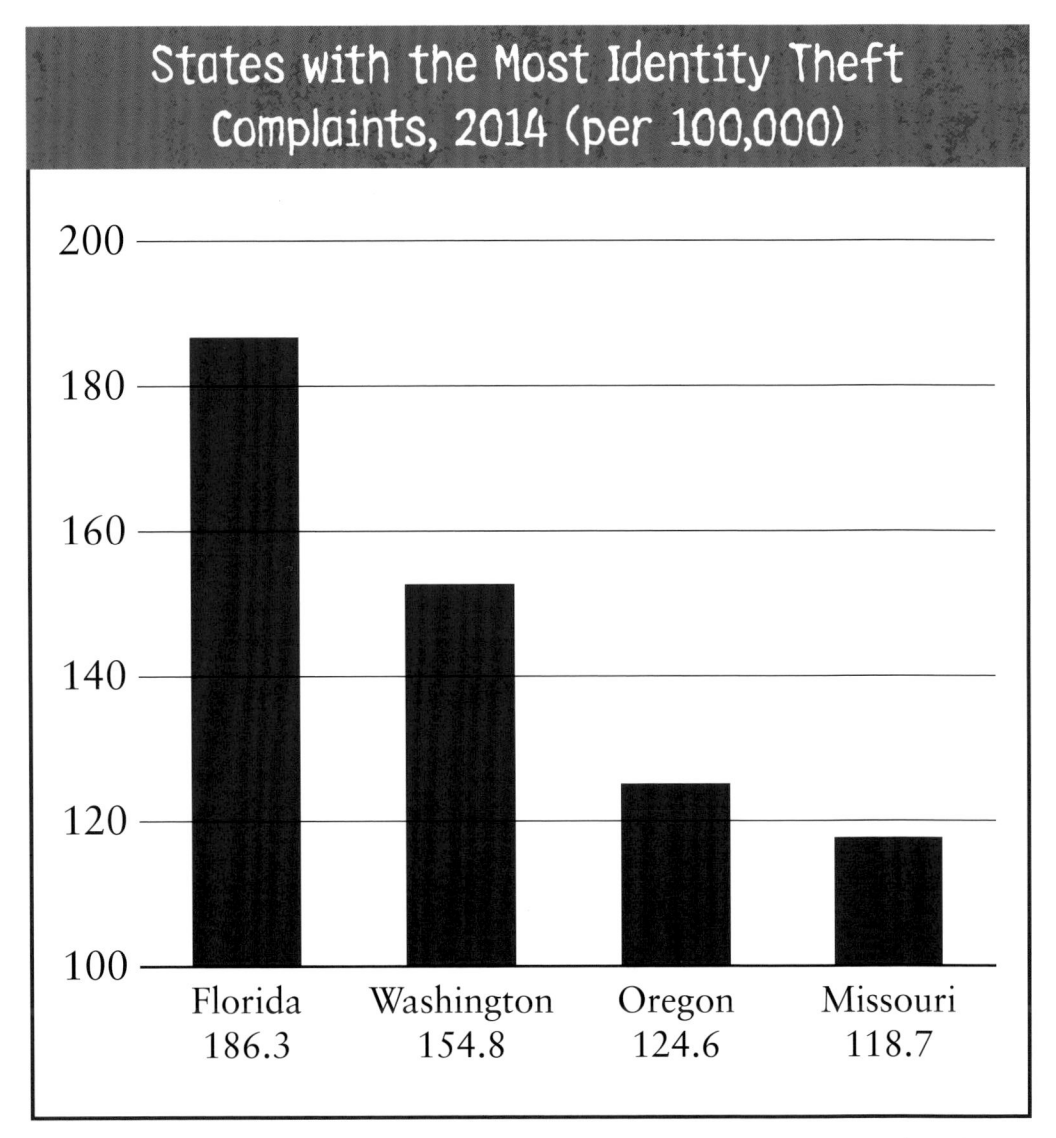

States with the Most Identity Theft Complaints, 2014 (per 100,000)

State	Complaints
Florida	186.3
Washington	154.8
Oregon	124.6
Missouri	118.7

According to data from the Federal Trade Commission compiled by USA Today, *these were the states with the worst identity theft in 2014.*

name appears on the check is located in Louisiana, the first numbers at the bottom of the check should be 11. If the check shows a different number, the identity thief has made a critical error. A sharp bank teller would be trained to look for a district number that matches the bank location; if it does not, that can be a major red flag—it could be identity theft.

Sometimes it is not the spelling or numbers that seem wrong, but the color or feel of a check. This is especially true with washed checks. No matter how careful a check washer is, there is generally a change in the texture of check paper that has been washed. Bank clerks who have handled a washed check describe the feel as fuzzy—distinctly different from the smooth surface of a legitimate check. These protection methods, though, depend entirely on the skill and experience of a professional.

Even the most organized identity thieves give in to the temptation to cut corners. "They go to the well too many times," said one investigator who has been involved in the arrests of several counterfeit check rings. "They may start out with the idea that they ... will only make the checks out for a [low] amount. But things go so well, they sometimes get kind of greedy."[19]

Lazy or careless thieves are almost always caught once they make a critical error. Some organized criminals travel from state to state, city to city, cashing and spending fraudulent checks and making victims out of dozens of innocent people. However, if a single clerk notices something wrong, or they make a mistake with a single check, they can immediately be arrested by local police.

All in the Prints

Though most crime scene techniques are not useful in identity theft cases, fingerprinting is one forensic tool that can occasionally be valuable. Many people do not realize that they leave their fingerprints on paper—including checks. They incorrectly assume that because a fingerprint is not visible, it does not exist. However, some of the most incriminating fingerprint evidence is completely invisible to the naked eye. These are referred to as latent prints, and they can sometimes be the key to solving a serious crime.

In some identity theft cases in which significant amounts of money are lost and cashiers are unable to spot the crooks in the act of passing checks, investigators look for fingerprint evidence. Many cases have been put on hold until there are more clues. A fingerprint on a bad check can sometimes provide just the clue investigators need. Because fingerprints are unique, they can often be used to find out exactly who has had contact with a surface. The biggest advantage identity thieves have is that they are anonymous. If they get exposed, they can easily be caught.

"What is found on a check or other paper is a latent print," explained fingerprint expert David Peterson. "The thing is ... the stuff that makes up a fingerprint, it soaks into the paper." By spraying a mist of chemicals on the check, the prints can become easily visible. It does not matter if the check is damaged or wet—there is almost always a chemical that will help. For example, the chemical ninhydrin is frequently used to bring out latent prints on paper. However, when ninhydrin does not provide a clear print, technicians may try silver nitrate, a different chemical. "We've got lots of choices—in all, 45 different chemicals for different situations. Often you try one, if it doesn't work well, you try something else that's more sensitive."[20]

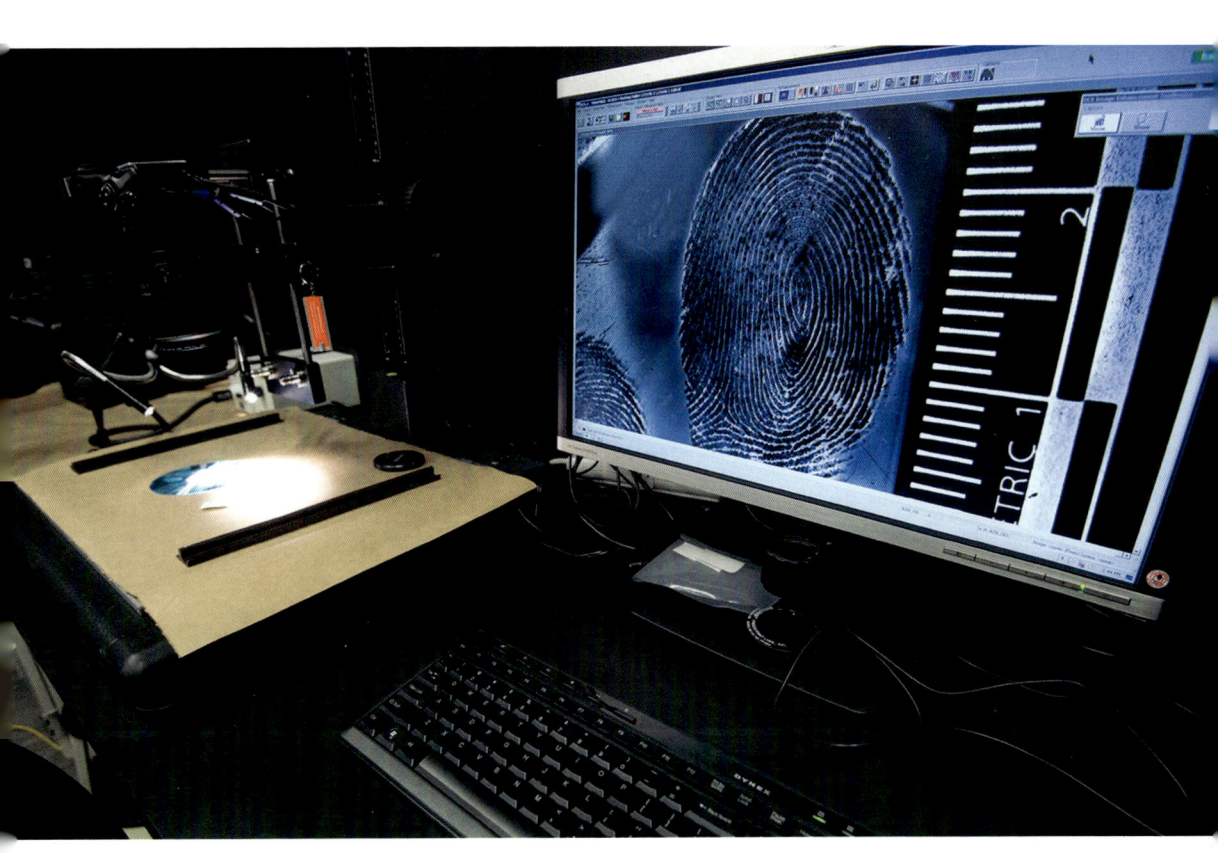

Especially in cases of identity theft, finding fingerprints can create a clear path directly toward a criminal.

Revealing the Fingerprint Clue

1. Wearing a latex glove so as not to leave their own fingerprints, a technician identifies the item that is likely to have latent, or hidden, prints. Sometimes, shining a special light on the surface of the check will reveal the presence of fingerprints.
2. The technician sprays a fine mist of a chemical called ninhydrin onto the check surface. Ninhydrin reacts with the oils and sweat left on the paper by the fingers.
3. The technician uses some device, such as a microwave oven or a steam iron, to apply heat to the paper. After a few minutes, any latent prints will appear in a bright, noticeable color.
4. The prints are photographed to have another record of the evidence. The fingerprints can be entered into a computer database and sophisticated matching software will return results.

Of course, many people handle a check during its processing, and it will certainly pick up many different prints. Fingerprint examiners often ask bank workers, tellers, or cashiers for their prints first so they can quickly eliminate them as suspects. With skill and a little bit of luck, investigators will find one print that does not match any of those people.

However, even the clearest fingerprint is of no use unless there is a suspect with whom to compare it. Prints from a bad check need to be compared with a suspect's prints. If there are no suspects, technicians run the print through a national database of known fingerprints called the Integrated Automated Fingerprint Identification System (IAFIS). The database contains the fingerprints of more than 66 million people. Most people know that fingerprints are routinely taken and scanned into the system when a person is arrested. Today, fingerprints are also obtained in a growing number of non-criminal procedures, such as applying for a driver's license, passport, or for government benefits. These fingerprints, too, are added to the database, increasing the likelihood that IAFIS will return a match for the print on a bad check.

Good, Old-Fashioned Police Work

Investigators emphasize that there is no single best way to solve check identity theft. "So much of the time it is a cooperative effort between different investigations," one investigator said. "It can be a fingerprint or just good old-fashioned police work, talking to people, walking around to stores asking if they've seen an individual we suspect is responsible for bad checks. You just never know how it's going to come together."[21]

One thing law enforcement officials are certain of, however, is that the technology that allows criminals to create very real-looking checks and empty the bank accounts of innocent people is a serious threat. "Technology is so good, and crooks know it. Forget about being ahead of them. That isn't happening—at least not yet. Right now, police are trying hard to keep up."[22]

Chapter Two
Identity Theft in the Mailbox

Identity thieves need a few pieces of key information to pull off their crime: a name and bank account information. A good source of this information is sitting right outside most people's homes, within reach of anyone walking by. It is the common mailbox. Millions of letters are sent to and received by American households every day, and many contain credit card or loan offers, checks, bank account information, and more. If this kind of mail gets into the wrong hands, a person's identity could be compromised.

Identities at Their Fingertips

Many crooks specifically seek outgoing mail that appears to be a bill payment containing a check. Once they obtain the check, they can wash it and replace the payee's name with their own or with a name on a fake ID. If they succeed in cashing the check, the money goes to them instead of its intended destination. However, stealing innocent people's incoming mail is the more profitable option for some identity thieves.

Many pieces of mail contain crucial bits of information about the intended recipient. Credit card companies send out millions of letters every day that try to get people to sign up for their cards. These letters frequently have some amount of personal information about the person they are being sent to, including a full name, address, and even a birthdate. Many people also have their banks send them physical copies of their account statements every month, and these contain valuable information, such as account numbers, balances, and other personal data. Some of the most common mail is bills, and these can contain a person's credit card numbers. If an identity thief got ahold of just one of these letters, they would be standing on a gold mine.

Unsecured mailboxes are a source of personal information that identity thieves would love to find.

Investigators worry about this. They know that mail theft is a major problem, and that it is a common method of stealing another person's identity. They say many thieves do not go after checks and money orders but search for information, such as a Social Security or bank account number, that they can use to open new credit cards in the victim's name. "The real money's in the credit cards," said one police officer. "That's what they want. We've arrested thieves who discard the little checks in the incoming mail. They don't have time for that stuff—that's small time. It's all about the ... cards."[23]

Interestingly, as law enforcement agencies began tackling the problem of mail theft, officials noticed a direct connection to another growing problem associated with criminal activity: addiction to methamphetamines, commonly known as meth. At first, no one associated the two criminal issues. After all, drug investigations and fraud investigations are handled by different divisions within police departments. Eventually, law enforcement agencies throughout the United States realized the connection.

The connection begins with the addictive nature of meth and its physical and psychological effects on the people who use it. First, meth is highly addictive. Many professionals, from counselors to doctors to police officers, agree that using meth takes over people's lives. Once they are addicted, it can be nearly impossible to recover. To continue using meth, addicts need money. The drug is expensive to acquire, and because the addiction is strong, many view the crime of stealing from mailboxes as a quick and relatively risk-free way to continue their drug use. Some thieves work alone, but many work with a partner. With one person acting as a lookout, the other can go through a dozen mailboxes quickly.

Drug Addiction and Mailboxes

People who steal letters are sometimes called "mail-boxers." These people steal mail from residential neighborhoods and hand over their haul to identity thieves. These thieves then sort through it for valuable account numbers and banking information. Mail-boxers are paid based on how much mail they steal. Mail-boxers are rarely just one-time criminals; they often work for the same identity thief dozens of times, stealing mail over a period of months or years.

Other addicts join together to form their own identity theft rings. While some do the mail-boxing, others sort through the mail. Others process any found checks for washing and create false identification documents with the personal information they find in the mail. Others, now armed with the victim's credit card information, activate preapproved credit cards without taking on much risk.

Investigators report that this sort of labor-intensive activity fits the profile of meth addiction. "It's a long-lasting high," claimed a drug counselor. "Twelve, fifteen hours—sometimes more. And unlike other drugs that make users feel spacey or … disoriented, meth produces a buzz, like you have all the energy in the world."[24] Richard Rawson, a

Stealing mail, either from an unsecured mailbox or someone's home, is a common way for criminals to get extra money.

methamphetamine researcher at the University of California, Los Angeles, said that ability to concentrate on detailed tasks makes meth different from other drugs. "Crack users and heroin users are so disorganized and get in these frantic binges, they're not going to sit still and do anything in an organized way for very long."[25]

Trash Is a Thief's Treasure

Mail-boxing is not the only way people steal letters. Some identity thieves would prefer to steal the mail a different way—by sorting through the trash. Few people pay much attention to their own garbage once it is out of the house, and even fewer think it could contain something worth stealing. Police, however, are well aware that what most people consider trash is valuable to an identity thief. Perhaps it is a credit card offer that did not interest the intended recipient, a discarded insert from a bill, or promotional material sent by a retailer to customers on a mailing list. All that trash has information that could be used to steal a person's identity.

Identity thieves know the value of garbage. Stephen Massey, who was arrested for trying to pass a fraudulent check, admitted to stealing garbage that he turned into more than $1 million. A businessman who had become addicted to meth, Massey first accompanied fellow addicts to a garbage dump, where they planned to scavenge for anything valuable to sell. It was the first time he had ever been to a dump, Massey recalled later, and the place was hardly appealing.

"I said, 'I'm not going to get dirty,' so I wandered over to a shed where the recycling was stored. I notice that there's a big barrel ... that's full of discarded tax forms from an accounting firm."[26] Realizing how much more potential value there was in information such as this, Massey began collecting paper trash from garbage cans and dumpsters. He soon developed his own large ring of identity thieves, making hundreds of thousands of dollars each year from discarded mail and other papers that innocent people had tossed out as worthless.

By the Numbers

27,000

number of fraud complaints investigated yearly by the U.S. Postal Inspection Service

Getting Caught

Though mail and garbage thieves are everywhere, they are difficult for law enforcement to catch. In fact, many arrests are made as a result of another, less serious crime. "We've caught them on a routine traffic stop—speeding, something like that," claimed one law enforcement official. "When the officer approaches the car, he finds it full of mail—literally full of unopened mail. At that point, he realizes it's something more than a traffic violation."[27]

In some cases, understanding the links between drug use and identity theft leads police to successful arrests. "Cooperation and communication between the cop on the street and [identity theft investigators] is hugely important," said a police officer. "Someone gets arrested in a drug house, and they find all these checks or credit cards, or mail, or whatever. So we get help from the cops on the streets, the ones who make arrests day after day."[28]

In many cases, police can catch an identity thief if the criminal gets sloppy or careless. If they target one community repeatedly, for example, the victims who live there will all report the crime to police officers. When law enforcement officials see a large number of complaints from one area, it is relatively easy to determine where the thief will strike next.

Video Evidence

The likelihood of catching a mail thief in the act is slim. Even if a suspicious neighbor calls the police about a stranger opening a mailbox or digging through trash, it would be difficult for police to arrive at the scene in time to investigate, especially in remote rural areas. Even in populated suburbs and cities, a mail theft call is rarely assigned priority over other crimes, so it is unlikely that an officer will reach the scene in time to arrest a suspected identity thief.

Law enforcement authorities insist that no one should risk their safety by getting personally involved in catching a criminal, even if that person is stealing their identity. For someone who has repeatedly been the victim of mail or identity theft, the best way to protect their identity is to further increase their own security. One easy way to deter mail-boxers is to replace an open mailbox with a locked one. Though a criminal could still break the lock, it would take much more time, and some thieves may no longer think it is worth it. In extreme cases, it is possible to install a hidden camera to take security footage from the area around the mailbox. If mail thieves are caught on camera or their vehicle can be identified, police can narrow down their investigation immediately.

Anticipating the Crime

Sometimes, police can actually predict where and when mail theft will occur. They may see, for example, that certain neighborhoods are reporting high levels of suspicious activity regarding the mail. Police may be able to determine other patterns based on the evidence at hand. For example, a thief or ring of thieves may be committing their crimes in an organized way, moving from neighborhood to neighborhood. By tracking the known criminal activity on maps, investigators can get an idea of the direction in which thieves are moving and where they are likely to hit next.

Police can also predict that mail theft is likely to increase on certain days of the month because bills and income checks are generally issued on

Surprisingly, post offices were the scenes of extensive mail fraud crimes in Southern California.

a fixed schedule. For example, Social Security checks to retirees are delivered each month on certain days; thieves know this and strike especially hard on those dates.

Sometimes, mail thieves are so successful in certain areas that they develop a false sense of security and fall into carelessness. With this advantage, investigators have had good luck apprehending them.

This was the case in Los Angeles in 2016. Over the course of about a year, investigators noticed that a large number of reports were made about missing or delayed mail in the same region. The pattern was clear—the mail in question was all processed through the postal offices in Southern California. Police discovered that several U.S. Postal Service (USPS) employees were committing mail fraud.

One mail carrier was charged with stealing mail to obtain victim's personal information. He used their information to order prepaid bank cards, which were then delivered to fake addresses on his route. As part of the same bust, investigators found about 48,000 pieces of undelivered mail in one mail carrier's home. While a post office may be the last place someone would think their mail would be at risk, it was actually the opposite.

By the Numbers

1,400

number of mail theft cases investigated by the USPS in 2015

Rings of Thieves

In many cases when a suspected mail thief is arrested, investigators know there are likely more people involved in the crime. Because identity thieves are often organized into extensive rings, getting just one suspect in custody is a valuable source of information about the ring's activities and the identity of other criminals.

Some suspects are quick to cooperate with police investigators, especially as part of a deal that reduces their own punishment. Police officers and district attorneys have the power to give one criminal a lighter sentence if they agree to give information that leads to the arrests of other criminals. If a mail-boxer is arrested, for example, they could be convinced to give up the leader of their identity theft ring in exchange for probation instead of jail time. Experts insist that the old saying about thieves having a code of honor is completely wrong. Many identity thieves would rather receive less jail time in exchange for providing information to police.

"Asking the Right Questions in the Right Way"

Occasionally, identity theft suspects are uncooperative after their arrest. Even if police have evidence that they committed a crime, the suspects may refuse to reveal any details about themselves or their accomplices. In cases like these, a police interview is an important investigative tool.

One officer said, "Never underestimate the power of the interview. Police can get a suspect to reveal a great deal, just by asking the right questions in the right way." She offered the example of a case of mail theft in Minnesota:

> It was a huge case. Twenty-five victims. Officers caught a check counterfeiter, who would print checks himself after stealing banking information from someone's mail. He'd take one of his checks to the bank and write it for cash. Anyway, he was caught after writing a bad check for $3,500.[29]

Based on an interview with this relatively low-level identity thief, police in Minnesota were able to make a number of other arrests that shut down the entire counterfeiting ring. This put criminals behind bars and directly protected the citizens of the state.

Finding Flaws

Professionals say conducting a good interview depends on establishing a rhythm with questions and being observant of the suspect's expressions and body language. Law enforcement officials are trained extensively in being able to read body language. A suspect's simple movements, such as itching their face, moving their head, or looking around, can give the interviewer a lot of information. By using a good rhythm in questioning, officers keep suspects off balance. This can cause a suspect to be tripped up in a lie or reveal more than they wanted to.

Officers are also trained to interpret the tone of voice suspects use to answer, the way they sit, and whether they maintain eye contact. These small details all provide an experienced interviewer with clues about whether a suspect is lying:

> You see some people with a nervous tic, they're shaking, or sweating. Of course, that doesn't mean they are lying. It may just be the idea of being in a police

A successful interrogation can be the make-or-break component in solving an investigation.

station, or talking to me. So I explore that. I ask a really straightforward question, like "What is your name?" And maybe questions like that, easy ones, they look up into space when answering. But when I ask a hard one, like about the bad check they just passed, they start picking lint or something off their clothing. You get a feeling, that's all. You start sensing when they are being evasive, or just plain lying.[30]

The First Victim of Identity Theft

Hilda Whitcher is reportedly the first victim of identity theft in the United States. She is famous for having the most misused Social Security number in U.S. history.

Whitcher was a secretary at E.H. Ferree, a wallet-making company, in Lockport, New York. In 1939, the company ran a promotion to show how Social Security cards could fit in its wallets. The company made up a fake Social Security card but used a real number—Whitcher's. Her actual Social Security number—078-05-1120—appeared on the card to make it look authentic.

The wallet, which was sold in stores throughout the United States, was a big hit. Though the example card was printed in red, was half the standard size, and had the word "SPECIMEN" stamped on it, people began using Whitcher's Social Security number as their own. In 1943, there were almost 5,800 people regularly using the number.

Eventually, the government canceled the number and issued Whitcher a new one. Still, thousands of people continued to steal her identity. In all, about 40,000 people reported 078-05-1120 as their Social Security number.

Using counterfeit Social Security cards, such as the ones shown here, thousands of identity thieves took advantage of Hilda Whitcher's personal information.

Using Government Resources

One important aspect of the investigation of mail theft is the USPS, a semi-independent agency backed by the federal government. Investigators appreciate the government connection because of the resources they have access to and because postal inspectors are extremely good at tracking down mail thieves. In 2015, more than 2,000 people were arrested by the investigative arm of the USPS.

Prosecutors, too, are glad the USPS is involved in identity theft cases. While many small thieves get off with a short jail sentence—or sometimes, serve no time at all—for possession of stolen property, possession of stolen U.S. mail is not a minor offense. Theft of mail is a felony under federal law, punishable by up to five years in prison for each count. Investigators hope that the threat of prison terms or large fines is a powerful tool in deterring would-be mail thieves and reducing this form of identity theft.

Chapter Three
A Closeup Look at Credit Card Fraud

As the world becomes increasingly digital, it seems as if almost everything happens electronically. That includes how many people pay for things. Most people use a credit card or debit card that is electronically linked to a personal bank account. While it makes the process of paying easy and convenient, it also exposes people to a huge security risk. Identity thieves with technological skill have discovered how to hack into accounts and databases to steal personal information. There are countless ways that crooks are stealing—and selling—data from people's bank cards and credit cards.

Paying with Plastic

When Jenny received her first bank debit card in the mail, she was delighted. She was living in rural Wisconsin, almost 30 miles (48 km) from the closest branch of her bank. She admitted it was inconvenient to travel that far just to get cash; with her new debit card, she could withdraw money from her bank account at any automated teller machine (ATM). "My adult kids would laugh at me, tell me to get into the 21st century," she said. "But I resisted for a long time. I didn't know how to use an ATM machine. But I finally caved and ordered [a card] from the bank."[31]

Jenny realized how convenient her card was almost immediately. She began using it not only to withdraw cash from the grocery store's ATM, but also to pay for gas and other merchandise where ATM cards are accepted, instead of writing checks. However, only three weeks after she got her card, Jenny could not find it.

"My husband said I probably left it in the machine," she recalled. "I

A Closeup Look at Credit Card Fraud 45

guess a lot of people do that—they get distracted or whatever when they're retrieving their cash and forget to take the card. He said that after a few seconds, the machine is supposed to 'eat' your card, so the next customer can't just take it—and so I should just call and see if someone could get it out for me."[32]

Jenny says she did not worry much about the card because she alone knew her personal identification number (PIN), the secret number each ATM cardholder chooses as

Almost as soon as people started using bank cards, similar to the one shown here, thieves figured out how to use them for identity theft.

a password. It must be entered every time the ATM card is used. She figured that even if someone else had the card, it would be useless because they did not know her PIN. The next day, however, Jenny learned from her bank that her card was not in the machine. She also was informed that her card indeed had been used over the previous 2 days to withdraw $400 from her account. If Jenny did not make the withdrawals, the banker explained, someone who knew her PIN did.

By the Numbers

7,472,540

number of U.S. consumers who had their credit cards compromised in 2016

Stealing from the Shoulder

Jenny's unfortunate situation is not unusual. Identity theft experts see many cases in which people's savings or checking accounts are drained by illegal use of ATM cards. Sometimes, carelessness with PINs gives thieves an opportunity. A cardholder who writes the secret number on the card itself or on a piece of paper in a stolen wallet or purse is giving a card thief everything they need to know to use the ATM card. Cardholders who choose a PIN that can be guessed from widely known personal information, such as a birth date or the numbers in their street address, also make it easy for thieves to gain access to their bank accounts.

Jenny made none of those mistakes with her PIN, however. Thinking back to the last time she used her card, she remembers a woman standing very close behind her at the ATM. "It's often known as 'shoulder-surfing,'" said one bank officer:

It's a pretty basic ... type of theft. Someone stands behind you and watches as you use the touch pad on the [ATM and] enter your PIN. A lot of people are so [focused on] what they are doing, they don't see someone standing maybe a little too close. So they've got your PIN, and then sometime in the future, your card is stolen, and they're in business. They have a card and a PIN, and they can steal everything you've got. People naively ... think they are safe even when the card goes missing, since their PINs aren't known. But crooks steal those PIN numbers every day. In many cases, there's nothing hard about it.[33]

A Closeup Look at Credit Card Fraud **47**

Shoulder-surfing can happen anywhere—at the ATM, the grocery store, or the mall. All card users should be careful to protect their personal information.

Easy Targets

There are many famous cases of ATM card fraud. One notorious case happened in the 1990s. An increasing number of bank customers throughout the United States had become the victims of a simple scam at their ATM. The scam was known to police as the "Lebanese Loop," named because it was started by Lebanese nationals living in London during this time. Experts say that, like every successful scam, the Lebanese Loop capitalized on people's innocence and gullibility. They did not realize they were set up to be the victim of a crime. As one woman described:

> I put my card in and a message came up on the screen saying the machine was temporarily out of order. A lady approached me and told me that this had happened to her the other day and what I needed to do was to key my [PIN] number in and then press cancel twice. I did this and of course no card was returned.
>
> I left the machine thinking that it had swallowed my card. But when I returned to [the bank] the following morning, my card wasn't there.[34]

Upset because her card was missing, the woman went to the police, who told her she had been scammed. They explained that crooks had most likely put a plastic loop-shaped sleeve into the slot in the machine where a card is placed. The sleeve prevented the machine from being able to read the numbers on her card, which prompted the machine to issue the message that it was not working. The "helpful" woman was, of course, a criminal. When the unsuspecting customer followed her advice to enter her PIN and push "cancel," the woman secretly noted the number the customer entered. After the customer left the scene, the other accomplices pulled the card and plastic loop from the machine. Armed with the stolen ATM card and its PIN, they had access to her money, and she was robbed of $500.

Other Kinds of Card Theft

Some methods of stealing bank cards do not even require the thief to be there. Tens of thousands of cards are stolen each year by thieves who use a device called a skimmer. The skimmer is a tool that can electronically read the identifying information encoded on the magnetic stripe on the back of an ATM card. When the card is swiped in a machine, the skimmer picks up the information and puts it in the hands of thieves.

In many instances, skimmers have been illegally attached to a legitimate ATM; a cardholder using the ATM is unaware that a skimmer is recording the data on the card during the transaction. In other cases, the skimmers have been disguised as ATMs themselves. The fake ATM

The green piece of plastic on this ATM is an anti-skimmer device. Anti-skimmers are meant to stop fraud before it can even happen.

is placed less than a block from a legitimate machine, which is falsely marked with an "Out of Order" sign that directs customers to the skimmer machine. Thieves who operate on this are taking advantage of their victim's innocence. Victims are tricked into thinking they are doing something safe and have no way of knowing otherwise.

Once criminals retrieve the skimmer, they have access to all the information collected throughout the day.

> [Crooks] can use the magnetic stripe information and make up their own debit cards. They can get a machine that reads the skimmer data, and [they use it to] manufacture a brand new card. Except it's my account numbers on their card, and my money they take. It's really astonishing what they can do, and nobody stops them.[35]

Protected by a Spelling Mistake

Investigators are able to solve some ATM crimes, but often not before a thief is able to steal thousands of dollars from unwary bank customers. In one case of a fake ATM set up in Maryville, Tennessee, bank customers benefited from the combination of an alert ATM user and a thief's poor spelling skills. The ATM had a sign on it informing customers that there had been fraud attempts at that location recently. As a safety precaution, the sign read, customers were required to use a nearby card reader first before using the ATM. The sign politely included the bank's apology for the inconvenience.

One customer, who stopped with her husband to use the ATM, was not convinced the card reader was legitimate. What bothered her most was a misspelling on the sign—the word "apologize" was spelled with an extra p. She thought a bank would not be so unprofessional. She told her husband her suspicions and called the customer service number at the bank.

Bank officials told the couple that they had made no such sign and warned them that the card reader was likely a skimmer. Though no suspect was identified in the case, one customer's alertness prevented more customers from being victimized. Experts say that sometimes preventing theft is almost as good as solving a case. Investigators are aware that there is simply too much fraud to solve every identity theft crime. However, when they are able to minimize damage before people are hurt, they view it as a success.

It can sometimes be difficult to tell a fake ATM from a real one. To ensure security, consumers should look for any suspicious signs and make sure no one can see them entering their PIN, like this picture shows.

By the Numbers

$16,000,000,000

dollars lost by credit card and debit card fraud in 2016

"It's Really Scary What You Can Do with a Computer"

Skimmers are not only used in fake ATMs and card readers. Criminals use smaller versions thousands of times a day in the United States to steal credit card information from unsuspecting victims. As with skimmed ATM cards, the stolen information is later transferred to other cards in a method known as "cloning."

The process of cloning is not complex. It requires a machine called an encoder, which can be purchased online and is not expensive. Using an encoder, a crook can easily transfer the information on a credit card to any other card's magnetic stripe. Many criminals make their own cards, which are hard to tell apart from real credit cards. This method has a high success rate, and criminals using it are difficult to catch.

One bank officer noted, "It's really scary what you can do with a computer and stuff you can order from the Internet."[36] Once a thief has a look-alike card, they can simply use the encoder to rewrite a card's magnetic stripe to exactly match the original.

"It's really amazing—in a bad way," said one victim. "Somehow there's this mystery about that magnetic stripe, you just take for granted that it's personal, it's private, and, most of all, unique."[37] Thieves take advantage of the fact that most people do not have the same technological know-how that they do.

A Quick and Secret Crime

Credit card skimming happens secretly and quickly, so a victim rarely has any idea that it happened. Security experts say it occurs frequently in restaurants, bars, and even taxis, and is alarmingly easy with the small skimmers available today.

A common scenario is similar to this: A dishonest waiter comes to a customer's table at the end of the meal, and the customer hands him a credit card to pay the tab. In a moment or two, the waiter returns with the card and the restaurant's copy of the receipt for the customer's signature. In that short time, however, the waiter has swiped the card twice—once on the restaurant's machine at the cash register and a second time on a skimmer in his own pocket. Police know that some waiters and waitresses carry tiny skimmers—which are easy to hide—in their pockets.

Other experts agree, saying that skimming can occur any time a card and its owner are separated. "You could be compromised anywhere," insisted one California criminal prosecutor. "Anywhere you give your credit card and you lose sight of it, it's possible to be skimmed."[38]

By the Numbers

100

number of cards one skimmer installed at a gas pump can capture daily

Unusual Card Activity

It is not surprising that because of the secretive and quick nature of credit card skimming, few thieves are ever caught. However, skimmers and credit card cloners do occasionally get caught, and it is often because of how they use the stolen card data.

Crooks often unknowingly help investigators when they become greedy. One way they do this is by overusing a credit card. Experienced identity thieves know that a credit card is not a permanent source of money. Customers who notice an irregularity on their statement—a large purchase or a purchase made overseas, especially—will alert the bank or credit card company of a fraudulent transaction, and the account will be closed. A thief trying to make a purchase on a closed account will draw attention. Even though police may not get to the store quickly enough, investigators can get a video image or description from store employees.

Identity thieves can also be apprehended when returning illegally purchased merchandise for cash refunds. This is a common way for some thieves to profit from their criminal activities. They purchase items from a store using a stolen credit card, then wait a day or so, and return the items. This allows them to get cash, which they can then use for whatever they want. However, many stores now have protective measures in place. These policies not only protect victims, they also help catch criminals.

Some large retailers will not allow a person to get cash back if they make a purchase with a card; the money has to go back into the account it was drawn from. If criminals return something at a store like this, they are actually refunding the victim. Additionally, if a person does not want to return something because they cannot get cash, it looks highly suspicious. Most stores have security cameras that can capture an image of a criminal, and if the person tries again, the police will have a major lead in the case.

Fraud Detection Software

Credit card companies themselves are able to first identify some cases of credit card theft. Though these companies have no way of knowing whether a person's card has been cloned or skimmed, they do have ways of analyzing transactions that highlight suspicious purchases. The most common method is the fraud detection software that looks through hundreds of millions of transactions daily, looking for unusual usage that might indicate identity theft.

Experts say that "unusual" is different for each customer. A purchase of a weekend spa treatment might appear on one person's credit card a

Outsmarting Smart Software

The software used by credit card companies and banks to detect suspicious usage was developed based on profiles of criminals' known purchases, ranking the probability of buying or not buying specific items. For example, identity thieves are more likely to use a stolen credit card to purchase hard liquor than to buy wine. Some identity thieves caught on to this theft-detection protection and began trying to outsmart the profiling software. Thieves started adding an item to their shopping list that did not fit the criminal profile and would not raise suspicion, such as a CD of classical music.

Software experts caught on to this trend in identity theft buying. They adjusted their profile tools, and since 2005, credit card purchases that combine expensive electronic equipment and a classical CD are now flagged. Every time identity thieves come up with a new way to outsmart protection software, credit card companies quickly add in a way to counter them. Protecting credit card users is an ongoing battle across the world.

---

few times a year, while another person has never spent money at a spa. A charge for heart medicine at a pharmacy could be normal for one customer but highly unusual for another. So, as credit card customers all over the world use their cards, software is tracking each purchase against other purchases each customer has made in the past. If something is red-flagged, the customer gets a call from the credit card company to verify the purchase.

Most of the time, a large or unusual purchase is completely legitimate. In those cases, customers simply tell the bank that they really did authorize the purchase. This gives customers peace of mind because they know the credit card company is alerted to suspicious purchases. It also helps the credit card companies because they lose less money to identity thieves. Many also offer other protections, such as spending limits. If someone set a single-purchase limit of $200, for example, the credit card company would call if they tried to charge a $250 purchase. This ensures that if their identity was compromised, they can cancel the transaction.

Follow the Money Trail

One key method investigators use to track a credit card identity thief is to follow the money trail. "It's basically numbers," said one official. "And anytime you buy something at a store, a gas station, whatever, there are lots of numbers generated. It's a footprint we can follow. She also claimed that, in such cases, video is frequently a helpful tool in spotting the identity thief:

> Let's say the card was used ... to fill up a car at a gas station; we can often look at the video for the time of purchase and get information there. Even though the card doesn't belong to the thief, the car likely does. So maybe we can get a license number from the video, or at least a description of the vehicle. And maybe the clerk on duty that day will remember something about the guy, or the thief on the tape will look familiar to us from other crimes. It really does happen, more times than you might think.[39]

Caught for Something Else

As with other types of identity theft, many credit card thieves are caught committing other offenses. If police pull someone over for a routine traffic stop, they might see complex electronic equipment in the car, such as skimming or cloning devices. In a case such as this, the officer can investigate further and potentially get an identity thief off the streets. Often, arrests based on evidence such as this are based on nothing but luck.

Las Vegas police, for instance, once had incredible luck when they caught on to a new trick used by identity thieves.

It was one investigators had never seen before, but one that they have been on the lookout for ever since. Police had been puzzled for months, wondering why so many of the drug users and other street criminals they arrested were carrying multiple hotel room key cards. At first, they assumed the cards were stolen and the criminals intended to break into and steal from those rooms. It was becoming such a trend that some reports claim that up to 10 hotel room cards would be found on a common criminal. This was strange, and police could not figure it out.

Hotel room key cards have a magnetic stripe that contains information, such as the guest's name and room number. When one Las Vegas police officer swiped one of the cards, he noticed that it held credit card information instead. The key card had been rewritten by identity thieves to serve as a credit card, using the account number of an identity theft victim. The thieves were then using these counterfeit cards to make unauthorized purchases all around Las Vegas.

Realizing that some crooks use rewritten hotel key cards to avoid being caught with someone else's credit card has proved helpful not only in Las Vegas but in other cities in the United States as well. Though the fraudulent cards can only be used at gas stations and other facilities where people swipe their own cards without showing them to an employee, they can still rack up large losses for identity theft victims. "It's pretty astonishing," said one security expert. "Really, the whole face of financial crime has changed. And it seems that the identity thieves are adapting very rapidly. We've got a lot of work to do."[40]

New Fraud, New Cards

Though credit card companies work tirelessly to improve safety and security with their products, up until recently, criminals trying to commit identity theft had an upper hand. In 2015, however, the balance of power shifted toward credit card users with the introduction of EMV microchip transactions. EMV stands for Europay, Mastercard, and Visa, some of the largest credit companies in the world. These corporations have been issuing cards with small, secure microchips for years. Cards with microchips offer an alternative way to access a customer's information by inserting the microchip into the reader. The old method of paying—swiping the card's magnetic stripe—has been notoriously insecure for a long time, but it was not until 2015 that American retailers led a push toward making microchip readers more common.

The reason microchip transactions are so much more secure is because information stored in the chip is more difficult for a potential thief to access. Magnetic stripes store a single code that is connected to a customer's single account. If a criminal steals that code, by using a skimmer, for example, they can access that account. Microchips, on the other hand, are so technologically advanced that they create a new code every time a transaction takes place. This is important because it keeps identity thieves away from a customer's accounts. Without the actual credit card, the data locked behind the microchip's secure codes is perfectly secure.

The weakness of microchip transactions is that they are so new. Some retailers still do not have even basic credit card readers, let alone the more advanced microchip readers. Still, for both consumers and investigators, the rise of microchip technology is a big win. Identity thieves trying to commit credit card fraud are finding their work more difficult every single day.

Chapter Four
Posing as Someone Else

Though check fraud and mail theft are serious issues, they are mild forms of identity theft. Not all thieves want money—some want to pose as another person. This is actual identity theft, which is a crime in which someone truly steals another person's identity. Identities are stolen for various reasons. The thief may want to avoid arrest or imprisonment. They may attempt to impersonate a legal resident or citizen to get a job. They can even carry out criminal activity and tie it to someone else's name.

In the most sinister identity theft cases, a criminal may adopt a false identity as part of a plot to commit violent acts of terrorism. This kind of fraud is dangerous—and violating. Victims feel that someone has taken something that is private and considered sacred: their identity. To really steal someone's identity, thieves need more than stolen credit cards or washed checks. Instead, documents of identification are the sought-after prize. A passport, Social Security card, driver's license, or a birth certificate can provide all the information needed to assume someone else's identity.

Easily Forged, Easily Stolen

Passports, birth certificates, and Social Security cards are the most important identification that U.S. citizens have. However, these critical documents are some of the easiest for identity thieves to forge. This poses a security risk because these documents could easily allow someone to gain entry into the United States when they are not allowed.

Technology has become very advanced, and with that, forgery has become easier. Thieves use high-tech computers, scanners, and extremely high-quality printers, and it has only improved their success rate. The Internet, too, has played a key role in the success of document forgers. Anyone can browse government websites to study the formats for official documents and re-create them in their own home. With a little bit of technical expertise and some relatively inexpensive equipment, even the smallest criminal could easily forge official documents.

The Best Documents

The most useful documents for an identity thief are birth certificates and Social Security cards. These are known as "breeder documents" because they can be used to acquire other important documents, such as passports and driver's licenses. For example, anyone can take a state driver's license test just by presenting a valid birth certificate.

Unfortunately, birth certificates are among the easiest to counterfeit. That is because there is no federal law regulating what a birth certificate has to look like. The United States National Center for Health Statistics has a standard form it encourages states to use. However, states are free to use whatever form of a birth certificate they wish. This makes it difficult for officials to determine the authenticity of any particular form. Additionally, birth certificates are issued by a vast range of authorities, from hospitals and home birth agencies to city or county registries. Few, if any, of these forms are exactly alike.

With a U.S. birth certificate, a person can apply for a Social Security card, another important breeder document. A Social Security card identifies individuals by a unique 9-digit number, under which a lifetime of tax records, government benefits, educational status, and other official records are filed. A Social Security number is required to legally be employed in the United States. Because of this, Social Security cards are one of the most commonly forged documents. They are in demand by countless undocumented immigrants seeking jobs in the United States. "It's the key that opens every door," claimed one man from El Salvador. "You need the Social for everything—to work, to open a bank account. They always ask you for your Social."[41]

Stealing to Work

Government-issued documentation is required for many aspects of life in the United States. This poses a problem for undocumented immigrants, or people who enter the United States without legal permission. Sometimes, people will commit Social Security fraud so they can get the proper paperwork needed to get a job.

It is estimated that 75 percent of undocumented immigrants use a

These are an American citizen's most important identification documents. They contain personal information that thieves can use to destroy someone's life.

fraudulent Social Security number to get a job in the United States. Some have been stolen from sources ranging from personnel files to online lists. There are thousands of criminals, especially people who have jobs working with the elderly, who are easier to take advantage of, involved in massive theft and sale of Social Security information.

There are countless counterfeiters who supply documents for a price.

60 Identity Theft in the 21st Century

Proper identification is needed to enter the United States legally. Once there, proper ID is also needed to work.

Their operations are largely concentrated in border states, such as California and Arizona, and in coastal states, such as Virginia and North Carolina. One Phoenix man who admitted he helps undocumented immigrants find people to sell them documents says it is a very easy process:

> A [human smuggler] will call and say ... "Can you help get this person some papers?" It's easy. I'll have a number for a guy and call him. We'll meet at the major intersection out here, say, in half an hour. I give him $50 or $100, whatever he's asking, a photo of the person, and a name. About 45 minutes later, he'll call me to come meet him on the same corner with the papers—a Social Security card and a green card [temporary work permit].[42]

Identity theft investigators emphasize that their job is far more difficult because many employers do not care if the workers they hire are legal residents with authentic documents. "In lots of ways, it's in [the employers'] best interest to have illegal workers," claimed a social worker in California. "They don't pay them nearly as much as they pay U.S. workers, so they spend less money on salaries. Many of the companies have sort of a 'let's pretend' attitude about the whole thing. But they know that many of their workers haven't got legitimate documents."[43]

By the Numbers

21,500,000

number of Social Security numbers compromised in a 2015 data breach of the U.S. government's servers

"It's Just a Number"

Many people do not see a problem with using someone else's Social Security number. After all, they argue, no one is using the number to steal money or hurt the original holder of the number in any way. One immigration advocate claimed, "It's a crime without a victim. I borrow your number, I get a job and work to support my family. I don't hurt you in any way. It's just a number."[44]

However, government and law enforcement officials, as well as many ordinary citizens, do not agree. Although it is true that many Americans citizens do not even realize that another person is using their Social Security number, the deception could cause enormous problems. A disabled man, for example, could be told the government will no longer issue disability checks to him, since he has started working at a construction company. Although the man is physically incapable of working construction, it is clear that someone reporting income under his Social Security number has been. As a result, the victim would suffer from not getting his disability checks.

There can be even more serious consequences if someone's Social Security number falls into the hands of a criminal. Police officers use this number as a way to identify people. A criminal could use a Social Security number as a breeder document, obtain a driver's license, and get that license suspended. If the victim is then pulled over by the police, they could be arrested for driving with a suspended license, even if they were totally innocent of the crime. The effects of using someone else's Social Security number are far-reaching and impossible to predict. It is much more than just a number.

A Threat of Terrorism

Identity theft has the potential to victimize people on a much larger scale. On September 11, 2001, international terrorist organization al-Qaeda attacked the United States, killing thousands of people. Federal investigators learned that some time during their stay in the United States, every one of the 19 terrorists who hijacked planes and crashed them into the World Trade Center, the Pentagon, and a Pennsylvania field had used forged or stolen documents. In part because of passports, driver's licenses, or visas obtained from fraudulent breeder documents, they were able to enter and remain in the country while planning the attacks.

Creating false documents caused a serious loss of innocent life. Investigators found Youssef Hmimssa's name in an apartment rented by al-Qaeda members in Detroit. In that apartment, investigators found plans for further attacks, with targets ranging from Disneyland Park to the offices of the *New York Times*. While Hmimssa denied being a terrorist himself, he acknowledged that he created false documents for al-Qaeda.

In his interviews with government agents, Hmimssa provided information about how easy it is for terrorists around the world to obtain fraudulent passports, visas, and driver's licenses. These documents allow international criminals to freely move to and from the United States. Hmimssa said he paid special interest to details to minimize any danger that the fraudulent

Posing as Someone Else 63

Despite the efforts of immigration and false identity experts, fraudulent documents can still go unnoticed. These counterfeit passports were seized in a major bust.

Defrauding the Government

The U.S. government is at the cutting edge of technological innovation to protect potential victims of identity theft. However, because most government agencies help private citizens or companies, it is itself often tricked. In 2015, nearly 50 percent of all reports of identity theft in America claimed that criminals were using personal information to get government benefits or documents. Because government offices have detailed personal information for hundreds of millions of citizens, some of that information can fall into the wrong hands. When it does, it is hard for the government to tell fraudulent activities from real claims because there are simply so many fake claims mixed in with authentic ones.

papers would be spotted. For example, he created his own ink for use in birth certificates that would stand up to the special lights that some of the most careful inspectors use to verify documents. Document experts noted that Hmimssa's work was frighteningly accurate. This exposed the extreme danger of the stolen identity business in the United States and worldwide.

Important Informants

With the sheer volume of illegal documents circulating in the United States, it is obvious that law enforcement agencies are overwhelmed. Even so, police and other agents have been trying to find new ways to identify and apprehend people who steal breeder documents and other identification papers.

As with many other criminal investigations, police rely on the services of confidential informants, often called CIs. A CI is a person with insider knowledge of criminal activity. They are sometimes actual members of a criminal community, but more often, they are average people on the street who secretly help police by telling them what they see, hear, or know about a case or a suspect. Confidentiality is essential: Once exposed, a CI's access to inside information ends and the CI risks retaliation from suspects or other criminals.

Cultivating CIs is a major part of identity theft investigations. One police officer explained the basic guidelines for finding these informants: "Basically, we were talking to people on the street, in bars and places where this guy was believed to hang out. It was nothing really high-tech ... it's just ... walking around, taking the time to talk to CIs."[45]

ICE officers protect the borders, which can help reduce incidences of identity theft.

Of course, not all informants offer their services for the good of the community. Some know that they can make a little money by helping an investigator with a case. "The department gives us a certain number of $20 bills for this purpose," an officer claimed. "The serial numbers are written down—it's very organized. So if we get some help from a guy on the street, we can give him a little money ... It's not a lot, but it's something."[46] These informants can truly impact the result of a case—or help get it started.

Because a large number of undocumented immigrants use stolen Social Security numbers, the Immigration and Customs Enforcement agency (ICE) frequently investigates identity theft cases. To expose companies that employ a lot of illegal workers, ICE commonly relies on informants with inside information to give them a tip.

What Undercover Investigations Reveal

Some identity theft cases have astonishing results, as discovered by agents of the Government Accountability

Office (GAO), an investigative arm of the U.S. Congress charged with tracking the use of public funds. In a type of special undercover investigation, groups of investigators set out to find out how difficult it was to get a legitimate driver's license with fraudulent breeder documents.

The GAO teams visited Department of Motor Vehicles (DMV) offices in seven states. Pretending to be identity thieves, they applied for driver's licenses using fake documents. Most were obvious fakes, such as birth certificates without official seals, or printed on regular paper instead of the special paper stock used by the government. Some of the team members handed DMV employees birth certificates listing a date of birth that did not match that on the license application. A few of the birth certificates had glaring alterations, such as an original name blotted out and a different name in its place.

Every one of the agents was able to successfully obtain a driver's license. What investigators found most alarming was that even when a DMV employee could tell a document was fake and rejected the application, the employee generally just handed the fraudulent papers back to the undercover investigator instead of calling over a supervisor to report it. They never confiscated the documents or notified law enforcement officials. Moreover, even if the agent was rejected, they came back later in the day and eventually got their application approved.

The findings of this undercover operation were shocking and frightening. GAO officials criticized DMV regulations and protocols and called for a massive reform of the system that allowed so many false identities to slip through. The ease with which an identity thief could obtain a driver's license is particularly alarming because a driver's license is the form of identification most often presented by passengers boarding U.S. commercial airplanes. After the September 11 attacks, the destructive potential of false documentation and stolen identities was made tragically clear.

Forensic Document Laboratories

Sometimes, identity theft cases involving fraudulent documents can be aided by more scientific investigative techniques. Although a forensic laboratory is not used very often in cases of identity theft, it can sometimes provide important information to investigators. For example, ICE maintains a highly sophisticated forensic document laboratory where seized forgeries and suspicious documents are analyzed.

While a forensic technician would normally not examine a suspicious driver's license, a suspicious passport might be analyzed because a passport allows a person to gain entrance into a country. Since the September 11 terrorist attacks, ICE and the Department of Homeland Security have been extremely vigilant about looking for signs of passport fraud.

The laboratory contains databases of inks, papers, stamps, adhesives, and other materials used to make or process legitimate passports and other documents in the United States and other nations. For instance,

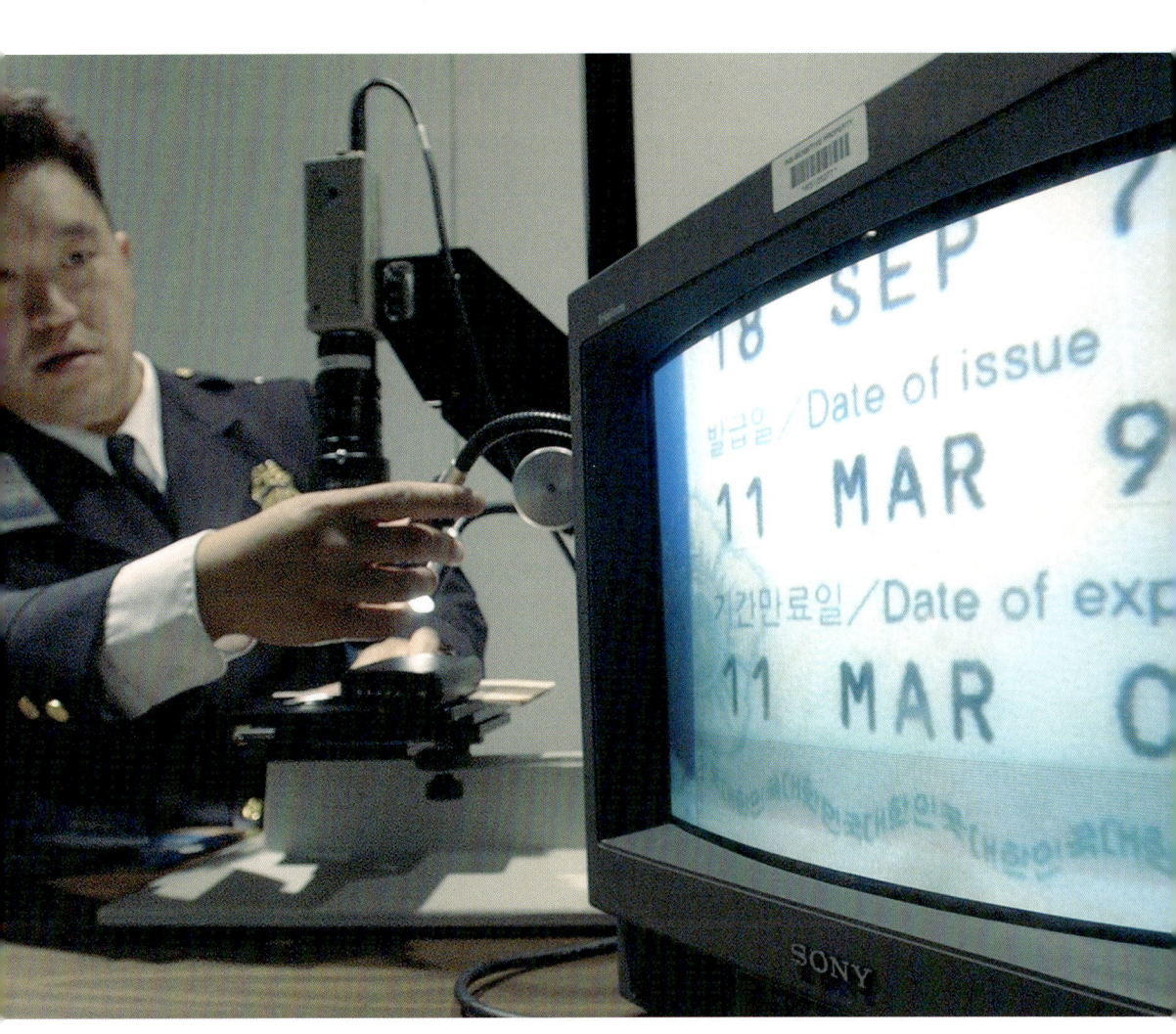

Law enforcement officers examine passports using magnification equipment so they can be certain of their authenticity. They look for the smallest details.

when someone presents a customs official with a passport that seems unusual or suspect in some way, forensic technicians use scientific tests to determine whether or not the document is genuine. Using expensive and high-tech instruments that can evaluate its components down to the molecular level, forensic examiners can be certain of a document's authenticity.

Of course, important U.S. documents such as passports have features that make them very difficult to forge or create on a computer. One feature is microprinting, a process also used by manufacturers of bank checks and paper money. Microprinting is the printing of text that is too small to be read by the naked eye. On a check, for instance, the line on which a person signs his or her name is really not a solid line, although it looks solid. Under a magnifying glass, it is revealed that the line is actually a long series of words. Microprinting is used on passports as well. Any official who has doubts about a passport can check areas that should have microprint. If the person has merely scanned a legitimate passport into a computer to create a new one, the microprinting would be lost, and the copy would appear to be a blurry line, not a string of distinct words.

The newest passports contain special ink, too. Known as color-shifting inks, they make the writing appear to change color as it is tilted back and forth. Blacks change to green, and back to black, for example. The secret to this effect is a series of layers of metallic flakes added to the ink. When the passport is tilted, light reflects off the flakes to create different colors. The U.S. government is the only customer of the manufacturer of this special ink. That means someone trying to forge one of the newest U.S. passports could easily be caught by an official noticing the absence of color-shifting ink.

The True Prize: An Authentic Document

Because of the difficulty of creating a fake U.S. passport, many identity thieves steal real passports and alter them. Stolen passports are readily available on the black market throughout Europe, the Middle East, and Asia. In addition, in recent years, authentic passports—American as well as those from other countries around the world—have been boldly sold over the Internet.

One way that identity thieves falsify a real passport is by using an extremely thin clear laminate over the picture and biographical data on the document. First, however, they chemically destroy the original photo so that it does not show through the laminate. This creates a double image. The laminate contains a new picture (typically a real picture of the thief or their client). While ICE officials do not wish to provide details about the method, they say that they have been successful in stopping such fraudulent passports because the laminate layer is never placed exactly over the original page. A slightly ragged edge where the laminate hangs over the edge of the page alerts a border official and the forensic lab can verify that it is a fake.

With new technology being developed for creating documents, national security experts hope they can use their own technology to slow down the use of faked copies. They realize that the stakes are high. Though illegal immigration is a danger, stopping common immigrants is not as important as finding and preventing an enemy from crossing the borders of the United States with an intent to commit an act of terrorism. Preventing identity fraud is a matter of national security.

Chapter Five
Computers, Cybercrime, and Identity Theft

Identity theft is a fast-growing crime. In a world in which computers and smartphones help humans handle everything from banking to shopping, identity thieves have access to a nearly infinite amount of personal information. All they need is an Internet connection.

Cybercrime is the term used to describe crimes that happen over the Internet and through computers. The FBI is on the forefront of combatting cybercrime, but it is getting more sophisticated and dangerous by the day. The most frightening part is that everyone is at risk, from government agencies to online shoppers to children.

Addressing Security in the Computer Age

Computers are essential tools in modern life, both for business and personal activity. In fact, experts say it is almost impossible to steal money, buy and sell stolen credit card numbers, or commit other types of business or identity fraud without targeting or using a computer. Moreover, criminals focus on cybercrime because it is relatively risk-free. Theft on a huge scale can be carried out from the thief's home, and they never have to physically confront a victim.

Unfortunately for law enforcement agencies, the risk of being caught and arrested is minimal, too. Although there are talented investigators with the tools necessary to solve such crimes, many police departments are overworked and underequipped. Typically, solving cybercrime requires many people working on many different computers at once, and most law enforcement agencies cannot divert the time and manpower away from investigations of violent crimes.

Though computers have changed the world for the better, they have also introduced a new type of crime. Hackers can steal information from around the world in seconds.

Another challenge in solving cybercrime is the time it takes between the moment when a crime occurs and when someone realizes a crime has taken place. Even the largest corporations tend to be unaware of being victimized. That is part of the difficulty of solving these crimes, and it is the nature of cybercrime.

It used to be that if I were to break into your safe and steal the $1 billion that your company had there, you would notice it was missing. Today, if I intelligently come into your [computer] safe and steal your intellectual property, you don't know that I've taken it, nor do you know what I'm going to do with it and how it's being used until you begin to see symptoms."[47]

It's the lack of confidence that people will get in online businesses. They will worry a company's website is not safe, that their personal information will be compromised. No one wants to feel unsafe when they shop. If those fears become increasingly common, that will hurt business in this country dramatically. That's the nightmare scenario.[48]

A Crime That Cannot Be Ignored

Even though computer identity theft poses such difficulties, investigators realize it is a serious crime and it cannot be ignored. Billions of dollars are lost to cyber-thieves each year as computer criminals steal corporate records and personal information about millions of credit card customers. They break into business and government databases to steal consumers' Social Security numbers and bank account information. They buy and sell that stolen identity data to other thieves, all with a few keystrokes.

Even with these serious threats, many businesses say there is a more ominous effect of computer identity theft than the massive amounts of money lost each year. "Most worrisome is the long-term effect of cybercrime," said one marketing executive.

By the Numbers

256

number of days on average it takes for companies to discover a data breach due to cybercrime

Corporate Crime

Some of the biggest victims of cybercrime are corporations. In a fast-moving business world, more and more information is stored online. This includes personal information about hundreds of millions of clients and customers. Though billions of dollars get invested every year to improve digital security, data breaches and

Computers, Cybercrime, and Identity Theft

cyber theft still occur frequently; 2017 is estimated to suffer more than 1,500 different data breaches in the United States alone. These breaches can affect any industry, including healthcare organizations and the federal government.

Sometimes, digital attacks directly steal money and put it into the criminals' bank accounts. Sometimes, a data

Data breaches are expensive for companies. In one of the most widely publicized breaches in history, hackers broke into Target's databases in 2013, compromising millions of customers' personal and financial information.

breach results in millions of people's personal information getting exposed to anyone who does an online search. Frequently, hackers break into digital archives because they want to extract information about people—including bank account and Social Security numbers and other personal information—and sell it to someone else. There are thousands of people across the globe who make a full-time living out of attacking companies' data stores.

When companies suffer from cybercrime, it is bad news for everyone. The company loses money (and potentially customers), consumers are at risk of having their identities stolen, and cyber security experts have to scramble to fix the issue. Because so much information is available almost instantly, hackers and digital thieves keep innovating new ways to get around even the most technologically advanced defenses. Unfortunately for a consumer, there is almost nothing that can protect them from a large-scale corporate attack. In the 21st century, people living in every corner of America store enough information online—from bank accounts to paychecks to Facebook profiles—for a dedicated identity thief to completely ruin their life.

Because large companies understand that they and their customers are highly vulnerable when they store information digitally, the field of computer security is one of the biggest industries in the world. Reducing cybercrime is a full-time job, and there are thousands of digital security firms across the globe that work to create new safeguards for common consumers. Companies pay these computer experts huge sums of money to protect their sensitive information because they know they have a duty to keep that information away from identity thieves.

Targeting the Rich and Famous—and Everyone

Experts insist that anyone can be a victim of computer identity theft. It seems to make no difference how wealthy, well connected, or protective people are—no one can guarantee their identities are truly safe. The case of Abraham Abdallah is just one example. Abdallah, an identity thief, victimized many kinds of people, from the world's richest celebrities to ordinary people. A 32-year-old New York restaurant worker, Abdallah became fascinated with *Forbes* magazine's annual issue listing the 400 wealthiest people in the United States. Using a computer at the public library, Abdallah was able to fake the identities (including Social Security numbers and other sensitive information) of about 200 of those people, including TV star Oprah Winfrey, director Steven Spielberg, and investment billionaire Warren Buffet.

Abdallah had few resources, but police say he was very creative. In addition to the profile data supplied by the magazine, he used the Internet to begin gathering information about his victims. The rest he was able to get by pretending to work for large investment firms. For this, Abdallah relied on his mastery of one of the most valuable techniques of a good identity thief, known as social engineering. "It's a type of manipulation," explained an information technology expert. "It's a way of getting people to reveal information without their being aware of it."[49]

Abdallah fast-talked secretaries and bank workers into giving him private and protected information about customers. He also created genuine-looking stationery with the name of investment banks and even had a rubber stamp made in the name of a prestigious investment firm. These small touches made his scheme very believable—and successful.

Sabotaged by Greed

By using a number of voicemail accounts in the names of his famous victims, Abdallah busied himself selling off investments and having money transferred to various accounts (which were also in his victims' names), as well as opening credit cards for himself in his victims' names. Because he was targeting people with extreme amounts of wealth, his fraudulent activities eventually gave him access to billions of dollars that belonged to other people.

He was caught, however, after six months—brought down by his own greed and the alertness of an investment banker. Abdallah decided to transfer $10 million from one victim's account at a large investment firm to a new, fake account in Australia. The agent was suspicious because he had seen five other requests for transfers come from the same e-mail address. Once the police were alerted, they wound their way through the tangled web of e-mail addresses and voice-mail accounts. They found Abdallah at the center of it.

Cutting-Edge Technology

Abraham Abdallah's crime occurred in 2001. His methods were considered complex back then, but today's technology is unimaginably more advanced than what criminals once used. Every time Abdallah had to interact with people in the process of getting sensitive information about his victims, he was at risk of openly exposing himself as an identity thief. Today's technology makes it possible to carry out major identity crimes without ever facing the victim.

Identity thieves have realized how much can be done in their homes or at their computer at work, armed only with software and a mouse and with little or no interaction with potential witnesses. They can hack their way into supposedly secure corporate computer systems, for example, and steal employee and customer data. They can then take that data to one of the countless anonymous Internet websites where this information is regularly bought and sold.

While some forms of identity theft are solved because of standard police procedure—following up leads, interviewing witnesses, and so on—the majority of these high-tech computer crimes require the expertise of a new, highly trained kind of forensic investigator. This new breed of law enforcement official utilizes the best possible technology to stop cybercrime at the source.

The Clues Are in the Hard Drive

Even when investigators think they have a suspect in a cybercrime case, evidence or proof of guilt is frequently difficult to find. This is where technologically advanced investigators

> ### By the Numbers
>
> # 60
>
> percentage of cybercrimes against large companies that are carried out within minutes

come in. "In cases of computer identity theft," said one security expert, "you're not going to have the kind of evidence you see in most crimes. If he is guilty, the evidence will be there all right, but it won't be in the guy's pockets or in his car. It'll be on the guy's hard drive. It's up to the computer forensics [experts] to find it. If it's there, believe me, they'll find it."[50]

Computer forensics experts are not only highly trained in using the latest technology, they are also investigators. The job requires more than just the ability to effectively use a computer. Though technological skills are a major part of a computer forensic examiner's work, they also need strong investigative skills. Computer forensics experts have to be able to follow a trail, find important evidence, and correctly identify the suspects. These are the same tasks that regular police officers do—except forensic computer investigators deal mainly with the virtual world, which is extremely complex.

In cases of corporate theft by employees, for example, investigations depend on a careful search of the inner components of the suspect's computer. In such cases, it is crucial that the suspect not be aware that his or her work computer is being examined, so investigators must work secretly, either at night or some other time when the employee is not present. In a process that looks more similar to a spy movie than a standard police investigation, forensic experts take photographs of the suspect's desk and computer before they begin work so that the workspace can be restored to its previous condition when the investigators leave. If they give the suspect any sign that they are investigating, the suspect could wipe out important evidence, making the process more difficult.

Because the forensic examination of a computer's hard drive is a long and difficult task, the forensic workers do not carry it out right away. Instead, they make a copy using special software that does not add or delete anything. That is important because if even a tiny detail is altered, the evidence will have a hard time being used to actually convict the suspect of a crime in court. A security expert explained:

For the same reason crime-lab techs are careful not to touch anything at a crime scene without gloves, [computer forensics workers] have to keep the evidence exactly as it is found. It's keeping the chain of evidence clean, not letting it become contaminated by any examiner or outside influence. Otherwise, that contaminated evidence is useless in court, and a guilty person could go free.[51]

FBI computer expert Mike Morris claimed that some of the biggest threats to keeping computer evidence clean are regular detectives who do not know how to keep digital evidence clean and safe. "They think they know how to use a Mac or Windows," he said, "so they fire up the computer and click through it. It's equivalent to walking through the crime scene."[52]

Leaving Behind Digital Clues

Finding incriminating evidence on a hard drive is almost always a long, challenging process. What investigators search for can best be described as digital footprints—clues that are left by the person using the

> **By the Numbers**
>
> **$170**
>
> average amount per person lost in a cybercrime data breach

computer that point to a specific crime. The evidence can be found either in looking at the activity of the user—which can be identified by an expert—or by the data found in files, folders, and programs.

In the example of employees suspected of stealing from their corporations, detectives and computer forensics analysts might work together to catch suspects in a lie. If employees said they knew nothing about the theft in a police interview, but their computers had files about their crimes, they will immediately stand out as likely criminals.

Sometimes, identity thieves put too much faith in the idea of deleting or erasing files. That can be a big break for investigators, who know that even when a file is deleted, it is never really gone. It is still hidden on the computer's hard drive—if the investigator knows where to look. Experienced professionals know that if a suspect has tried to delete their incriminating files, they are in big trouble. All it takes is a single computer analyst to access the hard drive, and they will be able to discover all the evidence they need to lock someone up.

This is confusing to inexperienced cybercriminals, who believe that if something has been deleted, it is gone. One security expert explained why this is wrong:

> *Lots of space [on a hard drive] is not used. Now, when you delete the file, that's like the index card that has information on where each piece of the file is. That's what you're really throwing away, not the file. Afterwards, you ask your computer, where's the file? It tells you it's gone, doesn't exist. [Police software] just goes in and reads the clusters of data in the hard drive. You'll find entire files or chunks of files still there—all of which you deleted. But it's really there.*[53]

The same is true for e-mails and Internet activity—computers record every website a user views and stores the information. That can be trouble for someone suspected of sending threatening e-mails, for example, while concealing their identity. A forensic investigator can use software

Cybercrimes happen on computers, and that is often how they get solved. Forensic analysts monitor computers, looking for evidence that hackers may be trying to get away with digital identity theft.

to get deep inside the hard drive and find the threatening messages, or at least enough information to prove that the suspect did send them using that computer, even if they tried to hide their identity.

> **By the Numbers**
>
> **47**
>
> percentage of data breaches caused by criminal activity

Hacked from Afar

Some acts of computer identity theft are stranger than others. In one case, a man woke up in the middle of the night, alerted by the noises his computer was making. "I thought it was my antivirus software running," he later recalled, "and I kind of ignored it."[54] As the noises intensified, however, he got up and looked at the screen and was astonished by what he saw.

The mouse cursor was moving by itself, darting around the desktop, opening files and appearing to be searching for something. He realized he was watching a crime in progress—a remote hacker had taken control of his computer and was looking for personal data. "I sat there as this person opened my [confidential files] and got my Social Security and credit card numbers."[55] As he continued to watch, the invisible thief began opening accounts to pay bills and new credit cards, all in the victim's name. Finally, he touched the mouse, and the activity instantly stopped.

Trying to figure out how a hacker could have obtained his information, the victim remembered going to an office supply store and using a computer there to check his e-mail. Forensic experts were able to track the computer used by the thief through its Internet protocol (IP) address—a code used by the company that provides Internet access to that customer. The company has records of a street address for each IP address.

In this case, the police traced the IP address to a man in New York City, who confessed to the crime. He had installed a software program in the office supply store's terminals that recorded every keystroke entered at the computers there. Periodically, he would return to the store and retrieve that information, which he would use to get into other people's computers. The software, which is often used by parents to monitor their children's computer use, was used for illegal purposes. Identity thieves take advantage of all kinds of software so they can trick and steal.

Impersonating Trust

The internet has opened up a world of possibilities for cybercrime. Just as Abraham Abdallah used fake letters and rubber stamps to make his fraudulent activities look realistic to investment firms, Internet thieves create genuine-looking e-mails to impersonate ones that come from trusted companies. The impersonation is so good that people rarely detect that it is fake and they may be tricked into giving the thief personal information, such as a Social Security or credit card number. This kind of computer scam is known as phishing.

There are millions of phishing victims every year. Because most people trust e-mails if they look correct to them, they can fall prey to an identity thief. "I got an e-mail from my bank," one victim recalled. "I thought it was my bank, I should say. The e-mail had the same design, the same way of writing the name, everything looked exactly right ... it told me my account information was being updated, and I needed to send my Social Security

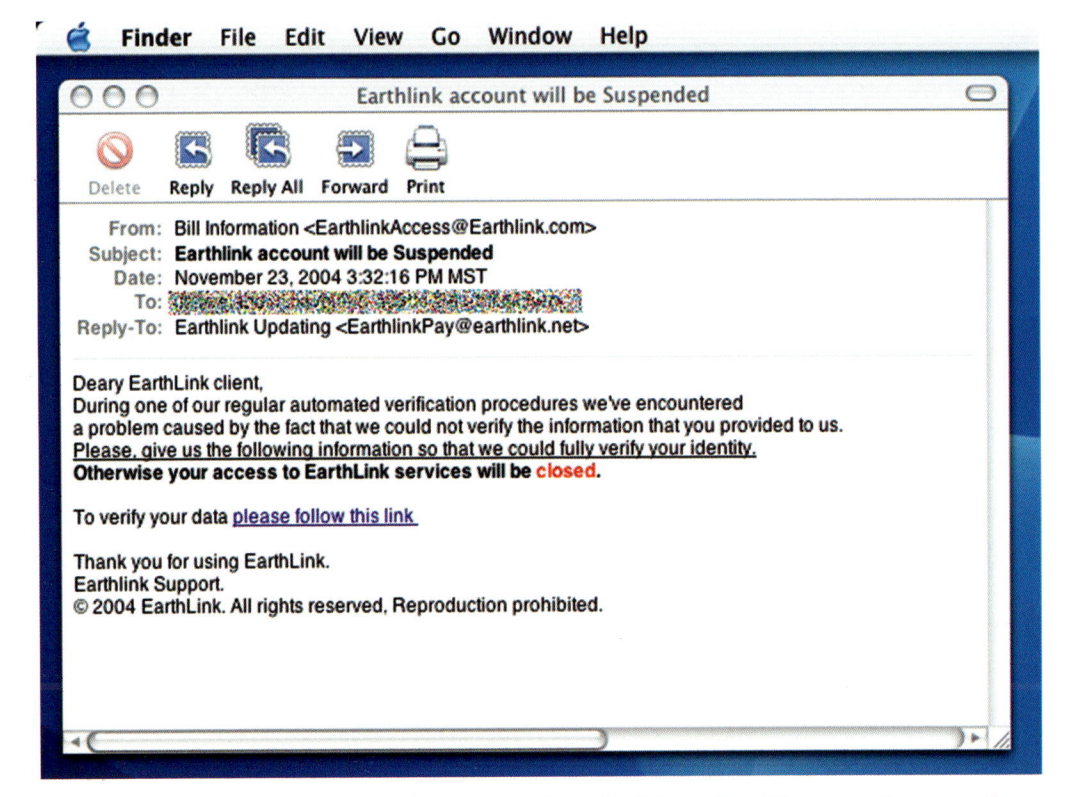

Phishing scams involve e-mails that are made to look harmless like any other e-mail. This is why people fall for scams similar to this one.

Can You Help a Prince?

As different phishing and e-mail scams have come and gone over the years, for more than a decade, one has consistently invaded personal e-mail accounts: the Nigerian prince scam. It works like this:

> The sender, who claims to be a government official or member of a royal family, requests assistance in transferring millions of dollars of excess money out of Nigeria and promises to pay the person for his or her help ... Those willing to assist are asked to provide their banking account number ... and Social Security number, birth date, or other personal information. Or they are asked to send money to the letter-sender for taxes and various fees. Victims never see their money again, and the con artist obtains the ability to empty their bank account and/or steal their identity.[1]

This trick seems easy to spot, but reports estimate that millions of dollars are lost every year to Nigerian prince or other similar e-mail scams. These e-mails are so common that they have become a widespread joke in movies, television shows, and books. Though these jokes show the victim as a gullible fool for falling for a Nigerian prince scam, in the real world, suffering from identity theft is no laughing matter.

1. The Better Business Bureau, "The Nigerian Prince: Old Scam, New Twist." Better Business Bureau. www.bbb.org/new-york-city/get-consumer-help/articles/the-nigerian-prince-old-scam-new-twist.

---

number and my savings account number."[56] He followed these instructions, which looked official.

Most victims of phishing scams eventually realize that they have been tricked. Nearly all banks, government agencies, and other online sources that deal with private information tell their customers that they will never ask for personal information. The easiest way to prevent a phishing scam is to keep that information hidden.

By the Numbers

156,000,000

number of phishing e-mails sent per day in 2016

Occupation: Computer Forensics Analyst

Job Description:
A computer forensics investigator's job is to collect and analyze computer-related evidence in a criminal investigation. Sometimes, this involves a computer in custody, but other times the investigator must locate the computer by tracing e-mails, IP addresses, or other digital information. In addition, an investigator is often called on to testify in any trials that involve the forensic evidence.

Education:
A computer forensics analyst will need, at minimum, a bachelor's degree in information technology (IT), computer science, or a related field. Some investigators also study criminal justice or have master's degrees in computer-related subjects.

Qualifications:
Specific training in IT is necessary for computer forensics analysts. They must have up-to-date skills in the latest computer programming skills. Also important are good reasoning skills and an ability to communicate complex topics to people who are not experts, such as juries in a criminal trial.

Salary:
The average salary of a computer forensics investigator in 2016 was $92,600.

A Crime That Is Difficult to Trace

In 2016, it was estimated that 80,000 people fall for phishing scams every day. Some respond to what appeared to be a bank message, others to a false retirement fund e-mail, and some to a fraudulent government agency. When they do this, they are willingly—but unknowingly—handing over their most sensitive information. Forensic experts say that phishers are experts at hiding their own IP addresses to make it difficult for anyone to trace them.

Though investigators have complex methods of tracing an IP address, it is often a waste of time. "You'll get a computer at a public library or [other public place]," claimed one. "And more often than not, the [phisher] will be operating out of someplace in Asia or Russia. There usually aren't enough resources

The Unsent E-mails

Computer forensics technicians find that most of their cases involve large amounts of money and complex technology. However, there are cases in which the motive is not financial gain and the methods are unsophisticated. In one case that took place in Minnesota, a woman filed a lawsuit against her boss, a 31-year-old married man, because she claimed he had sexually harassed her. The boss denied the charge and accused the female employee of harassing him. To prove his point, he produced printouts of several inappropriate e-mails she had sent to him. He further said that she was angry with him for refusing her advances, which was why she was suing him.

Investigators looked at the man's computer, but nowhere among the e-mails could they find the messages he showed them. They questioned how that could be possible. The man had showed them the explicit e-mails. What investigators found was that the man had written the e-mails to himself, pretending to be the woman. He never actually sent them, but printed them out, so it looked as though they were real. That evidence proved he had lied.

---

to pursue an investigation like that, not unless it was a matter of national security or something."[57]

All computer security experts agree that the best way to stay protected from cybercrime is to prevent it at the source. However, millions of people all across the world are relatively ignorant of how computers and scams work. One investigator said, "I wish we had more money to educate. We could eliminate 99 percent of this stuff if people just knew what to do to be safer. I mean, we lock our houses, we lock our cars, but we get on a computer, and we go into freefall ... we share information like crazy."[58]

The Underbelly of the Internet

Occasionally, investigators can track an identity thief in the process of selling the stolen data. To sell information, thieves rely on the countless message boards and chat rooms where the Internet's black market flourishes. In these unmonitored places, stolen credit information is bought and sold, Social Security numbers get passed around, and criminals make profits. These sites are impossible to keep track of, so much of the online world is lawless.

Some forensic investigators try to monitor such message boards and chat rooms, hoping to gather clues about who the identity sellers

Computers, Cybercrime, and Identity T...

are. Several investigators have taken part in undercover operations in which they try to impersonate a potential buyer. However, successfully completing these operations is difficult, partly because chat rooms move around quite often, but more because of the skill and experience of the criminals. If an undercover agent makes a single slip-up, the investigation is over. The criminals will flee to other, more protected sites.

However, police patience has paid off. In an undercover investigation code-named Operation Firewall, federal government agents and computer forensics experts watched their screens as various members of an

Cybercrimes, especially online identity theft, have become so threatening that even the FBI has gotten involved. Wanted posters are released to help catch dangerous online hackers and criminals.

organized identity theft network talked online. Though the members would typically take time to use screen names to cover their IP addresses, at one time, someone logged on from an unsecured computer.

This was the break investigators needed. They were able to trace the criminal through his IP address. Once he was caught, he was willing to help agents identify other members of his network. This led to a total of 28 identity theft criminals in 8 states and several countries being arrested, and investigators were able to get a closer look at how such networks are organized.

Future Identity Protection

It is no secret: Identity theft is on the rise and it has been for decades. Human interest in and use of technology is only contributing to the problem, and police are struggling to keep up. As technology assists people in more aspects of managing their lives, they are exposing even more of their personal information to potential scammers with malicious intentions.

Nobody knows for sure what the future of identity theft and cybercrime looks like. Every case that investigators look into is important, whether or not it eventually gets solved. Information learned in the investigations or arrest of an identity thief can help law enforcement in the future. Law enforcement officials are constantly revising and adapting their strategies to keep up with sophisticated methods that identity thieves invent. Some experts are cautiously optimistic about the future. They say the creation of new forensic methods, such as software that can red-flag purchases made by potential identity thieves, are evidence that they may someday be able to get the upper hand with these cyber criminals.

It is not entirely up to law enforcement, though. Consumers and computer users have a responsibility to protect their information and reduce the risk of identity theft. Consumers can pay for identity protection services that alert them to suspicious activity. One of the best tools to fight identity theft, however, is common sense. Government agencies and businesses will never ask for sensitive information. Personal information should never be accessed using an unsafe computer, such as a computer in a public library. Finally, consumers must always be on the defensive. It is impossible to tell for sure who is on the other end of the computer.

Is fighting digital identity theft a battle that will be impossible to win? Organized rings of identity thieves operating out of foreign countries are difficult to combat. Combined with their sophisticated technology, these identity thieves always seem to be one step ahead of law enforcement with their evolving skills. One security expert claimed that criminals adjust faster than law enforcement can keep up. "These threats are constantly evolving and changing," he said. "I don't think we're on top of it."[59] No one knows what the future holds, but if law enforcement can find out before identity thieves, they may have a chance to greatly reduce this crime.

Chapter Six
Staying Safe

Since the Internet became widespread in the 1990s, the digital world has helped humankind advance in uncountable ways. In many respects, life has gotten simpler for hundreds of millions of people. Paychecks can be automatically deposited, funds can be transferred from a mobile phone, and online storage space can hold every piece of a person's personal information. With increased convenience, however, comes increased danger.

For almost as long as the Internet has been around, there have been hackers, attackers, and scammers trying to get access to other people's money and information online. Anticybercrime task forces, whether privately owned or run by the government, have their hands full in fighting against this cunning and intelligent new breed of identity thieves. It seems that with every step taken by computer security experts is still one step behind the skills of hackers and cybercriminals. Despite the risks of putting personal information online, the Internet is a part of most people's daily life. It is important that all Internet users understand basic security if they want to be protected.

Starting with the Basics

There are a number of easy things that can significantly help prevent identity theft online. First and foremost is making sure that any time an Internet user puts information online, they are only giving it to a reputable and trustworthy site. There are countless cases of someone having their identity stolen because they entered their credit card or bank account information into an online shopping site that was not secure. Most browsers will tell users when they are visiting a site that looks suspicious, and these warnings can save people thousands of dollars.

Another important part of online safety is finding and using effective antivirus software for personal computers. This kind of protective software can prevent someone from stealing personal information directly from the hard drive of home devices. However, there are thousands of companies that produce antivirus programs. This makes it difficult to recognize which company is truly offering the best service. Moreover, some scammers and identity thieves will sell corrupted antivirus software that can steal someone's information when they install it. As with most digital security concerns, individuals can help protect themselves by using common sense and doing research about who to trust.

It is also dangerous to use a computer that is not trusted. Public computers, such as those in libraries or schools, are not the appropriate places to access the Internet for private or sensitive uses. Unlike with a private computer, people who use public computers have no idea who will be accessing it after they leave. If someone used a library computer to do some online banking, for example, then forgot to log out of their personal account, the next person to use the computer would have full access to their funds. Many cases of identity theft start with a person simply forgetting to sign out with a single extra click. The best way to avoid this kind of potential identity theft is to use public computers only for general browsing.

Stopping Cybercrime in Social Media

Similarly to the Internet in general, the rise of social media has brought both positives and negatives. Using tools such as Instagram, Facebook, and Snapchat, billions of people in all corners of the world are able to connect with family and friends—and sometimes, identity thieves. Because a large portion of people using social media sites post personal information—including photographs, their address, their birthdate, and more—cybercriminals can have an easy time taking advantage of someone. That is why it is important to keep as much private information hidden as possible.

Facebook, one of the largest online forces in the modern world, has a wide variety of privacy tools to help keep someone's identity safe. Users can decide who gets to see their profile, posts, friend lists, and other personal information. It is important that everyone who uses Facebook and other social networking sites knows the dangers of sharing personal information, accepting requests from people they do not know, and the risks of having their identity stolen. This is especially true

21st-Century Fishing

Inspired by a 2010 film and its long-running television adaptation, the world was introduced to a new term: catfishing. This refers to someone setting up an online profile pretending to be someone else to trick people into starting a romantic relationship with them. While not all cases of catfishing are identity theft, there have been many cases where an impersonator has based their fake online persona on someone else's information. Though copying someone's profile picture may seem relatively harmless, some of these catfish actually benefit financially from their lies.

After making contact, a catfishing identity thief will try to make their victim trust them. These scammers are experts in manipulating others to do what they want. After weeks, months, or years of earning someone's trust and affection online using a fake identity, a catfish will ask the other person to send them some money. In extreme cases, the catfish may be trying to use their fake online account to steal yet another identity—this time from their catfishing victim. This is just one reason why it is important to verify any friend requests or messages on social media sites.

with respect to personal images, as a potential identity thief can copy and steal dozens of a user's photographs to impersonate them. Even with the helpful privacy tools that social media sites offer, all users need to be aware that anything that goes online is being exposed to potentially billions of other people on the Internet.

Cyber security experts urge people who use Instagram and other sites to keep personal information sharing to a minimum. For example, someone may think that posting their address is harmless. If they are targeted by a cybercriminal, however, that person could call a bank, use that address to pretend to be the victim, and open a new account in their name. Even the smallest piece of personal information can mean the difference between a successful or a failed identity theft attempt. Instead of posting a home address to a public profile, it is much more secure to only share that information with trusted people privately. Computer experts also recommend that people turn their privacy settings to the maximum level, which generally means that only verified and accepted friends can see anything they post online. This is a simple way to fix a potentially major problem.

Adapting Protection

Internet users can do a lot to protect their personal information and help prevent identity theft, but the fact remains that hackers are dedicated and intelligent. Even if someone has followed the strictest personal privacy standards, all it would take is a single data breach, at a bank or grocery store, for example, for their identity to be stolen. For this reason, the industry of cyber protection is one of the fastest growing in the world. Unlike many professions, people working in computer security are required to quickly and frequently adapt their skills to entirely new threats. Because it is nearly impossible to predict how cybercrime is going to attack next, some of the world's largest digital companies have been coming up with innovative ways to advance computer security.

Google, which has long been at the forefront of digital technology, made an unexpected but important announcement in 2017: They had cracked one of the Internet's oldest security programs, Secure Hash Algorithm 1 (SHA-1). While it seems strange to hear a reputable company was working to break into a security program, Google actually did it to improve online security for everyone in the world. While SHA-1 is no longer widespread because other, more secure methods have been in use for years, there are still many sites that use it to protect information. What Google wanted to do, they stated, was to prove that SHA-1 was not secure, which would force digital companies to adopt new protection methods. This has an added benefit of encouraging makers of security similar to SHA-1 to recognize the failures of that code. This way, when new security procedures are being created, they will be much stronger and more dependable than older programs.

Researchers at top universities for computer science are constantly coming up with new theories and ideas for how to strengthen digital information. While some never make it out of the classroom, there are dozens of new and revolutionary concepts that are being discussed all around the globe. The need to reduce cybercrime—especially identity theft—is something that every country in the world can agree on.

Notes

Introduction: An Invisible Crime

1. Brendan Peterson, telephone interview by the author of *Identity Theft*, December 1, 2006.
2. Peterson, December 1, 2006.
3. Terry, telephone interview by author of *Identity Theft*, November 16, 2006.
4. Samantha, interview by the author, of *Identity Theft*, Minneapolis, MN, November 8, 2006.
5. Terry, interview by the author, Minneapolis, MN, November 16, 2006.
6. Bob, telephone interview by the author of *Identity Theft*, January 7, 2007.
7. Quoted in Daniel Wolfe, "ID Theft Group Members Say Collaboration Helps," *American Banker*, February 17, 2005. www.americanbanker.com/news/id-theft-group-members-say-collaboration-helps.
8. Donna, interview by the author of *Identity Theft*, Minneapolis, MN, January 15, 2007.

Chapter One: Bad Business at the Bank

9. Terry, November 16, 2006.
10. Terry, November 16, 2006.
11. Raymond, interview by the author of *Identity Theft*, Bloomington, MN, November 29, 2006.
12. Steve Kincaid, interview by the author of *Identity Theft*, Minneapolis, MN, March 10, 2006.
13. Vicki Colliander, interview by the author of *Identity Theft*, Lake Elmo, MN, March 3, 2006.
14. Joleen, telephone interview by the author of *Identity Theft*,

St. Paul, MN, November 11, 2006.
15. Colliander, March 3, 2006.
16. Sarah Nasset, interview by the author of *Identity Theft*, St. Paul, MN, December 12, 2006.
17. Charles, telephone interview by the author of *Identity Theft*, January 6, 2007.
18. Nasset, December 12, 2006.
19. Terry, November 16, 2006.
20. David Peterson, interview by the author of *Identity Theft*, St. Paul, MN, April 20, 2005.
21. Nasset, December 12, 2006.
22. Nasset, December 12, 2006.

Chapter Two:
Identity Theft
in the Mailbox

23. Terry, November 16, 2006.
24. Irene, telephone interview, December 13, 2006.
25. Quoted in John Leland, "Meth Users, Attuned to Detail, Add Another Habit: ID Theft," *New York Times*, July 11, 2006. www.nytimes.com/2006/07/11/us/meth-users-attuned-to-detail-add-another-habit-id-theft.html.
26. Quoted in Stephen Mihm, "Dumpster-Diving for Your Identity." *New York Times*, December 21, 2003. www.nytimes.com/2003/12/21/magazine/dumpster-diving-for-your-identity.html.
27. Kincaid, March 10, 2006.
28. Nasset, December 12, 2006.
29. Nasset, December 12, 2006.
30. Nasset, December 12, 2006.

Chapter Three:
A Closeup Look
at Credit Card Fraud

31. Jenny, interview by the author of *Identity Theft*, Minneapolis, MN, December 26, 2006.
32. Jenny, December 26, 2006.
33. Steve, telephone interview by the author, January 16, 2007.
34. Quoted in "Beware of Crooks

Disabling ATM Machines to Get Your Card," TruthorFiction.com. www.truthorfiction.com/lebaneseloop.
35. Lori, telephone interview by the author of *Identity Theft*, January 6, 2007.
36. Rob, telephone interview by the author of *Identity Theft*, January 16, 2007.
37. Lori, January 6, 2007.
38. Quoted in "Is Your Credit Card Being Skimmed?," CBS News, December 6, 2002. www.cbsnews.com/news/is-your-credit-card-being-skimmed.
39. Nasset, December 12, 2006.
40. Norah, telephone interview by the author of *Identity Theft*, January 18, 2007.

Chapter Four: Posing as Someone Else

41. Quoted in Franco Ordonez, "Phony IDs luring illegal Immigrants," *Charlotte Observer*, April 25, 2006.
42. Quoted in Faye Bowers, "ID theft poses challenge to immigration officials," *The Seattle Times*, December 14, 2006. www.seattletimes.com/nation-world/id-theft-poses-challenge-to-immigration-officials/ .
43. Marcia, telephone interview by the author of *Identity Theft*, January 3, 2007.
44. Arnoldo, telephone interview by the author of *Identity Theft*, January 4, 2007.
45. Nasset, December 12, 2006.
46. Nasset, December 12, 2006.

Chapter Five: Computers, Cybercrime, and Identity Theft

47. Quoted in Kathryn Jones, "Cybersleuths," *Texas Monthly*, August 2000. www.texasmonthly.com/articles/cybersleuths.
48. Barbara Kramer, telephone interview by the author of

Identity Theft, January 26, 2007.
49. Firasat Khan, interview by the author of *Identity Theft,* Minneapolis, MN, December 15, 2006.
50. Norah, January 18, 2007.
51. Peter Olsen, telephone interview by the author of *Identity Theft,* January 3, 2007.
52. Quoted in Jones, "Cybersleuths."
53. Khan, December 15, 2006.
54. Quoted in Lisa Napoli, "The Kinko's Caper: Burglary by Modem," *New York Times,* August 7, 2003. www.nytimes.com/2003/08/07/technology/the-kinko-s-caper-burglary-by-modem.html.
55. Quoted in Lisa Napoli, "The Kinko's Caper."
56. Lon, interview by the author of *Identity Theft,* Burnsville, MN, November 28, 2006.
57. Norah, January 18, 2007.
58. Nasset, December 12, 2006.
59. Roy, telephone interview by the author of *Identity Theft,* April 16, 2007.

For More Information

Books

Abramovitz, Melissa. *Online Predators.* San Diego, CA: ReferencePoint Press, 2017. This work offers a look at the type of aggressive criminal activity that occurs over the Internet, including identity theft.

Entingoff, Kim. *Navigating Cyberspace.* Broomall, PA: Mason Crest Publishers, 2015. This book is a detailed source of information on the threats of cyberspace, including identity theft and online bullying.

Hanel, Rachael. *Identity Theft.* New York, NY: Marshall Cavendish Benchmark, 2011. Offering an examination of identity theft and its legal consequences, this book is a great resource.

Roesler, Jill. *Online Identity and Privacy: 12 Things You Need to Know.* Mankato, MN: 12-Story Library, 2016. Detailed and well researched, this book is a comprehensive look at online privacy and identity theft.

Whiting, Jim. *Identity Theft.* San Diego, CA: ReferencePoint Press, 2013. This book offers a modern and close examination of identity theft in the 21st century.

Websites

Federal Trade Commission (www.identitytheft.gov)
Hosted by the American federal government, this site has comprehensive information on identity theft and resources for victims.

Identity Theft Resource Center (www.idtheftcenter.org/id-theft/teen-space.html)
This useful site has important information about identity theft and is perfect for a young audience.

National Crime Prevention Council (www.ncpc.org/programs/teens-crime-and-the-community/publications-1/preventing-theft/contact)
Focusing on educating young internet users, this site has tips and facts that can keep them safe online.

TransUnion—Identity Theft (www.transunion.com/identity-theft)
One of the three major credit-reporting bureaus offers helpful information on identity theft and identity protection on this site.

USA.gov—Identity Theft (www.usa.gov/identity-theft)
Created by the U.S. government, this site has resources and tips for preventing identity theft.

Index

A
Abagnale, Frank, Jr., 21
Abdallah, Abraham, 74–75, 81
addicts, 34, 36
al-Qaeda, 62
amount lost to fraud, 9
antivirus software, 80, 89
Arizona, 61
ATM card crimes
  Lebanese Loop con game, 48
  shoulder-surfing and, 23, 46–47
  skimming and, 48–52
  solving, 53–56

B
bank account numbers, 16, 34
bank tellers, 25, 28
birth certificates, 57–58, 64, 66
black markets, 68, 84
body language, 40
border states, 61
breeder documents, 58, 62, 64, 66

C
California, 36, 38–39, 52, 61
Catch Me If You Can (film), 21
catfishing, 90
check fraud
  amount of, 22
  defrauding checking accounts, 23–25
  microprinting and, 68
  solving, 28–31
  stealing checks, 16–17
  washing checks, 22–23, 28
classical CDs and theft, 54
cloning credit cards, 51, 53, 55
color-shifting inks, 68
computers
  databases of fingerprints, 30
  digital footprints on, 77
  forensic experts, 68, 76–77, 80, 83
  fraud detection software, 53–54
  increased use of, 7, 15
  manufacturing ID with, 58, 61
  used to clone credit cards, 51, 53, 55
  using to alter checks, 23–25
  See also cybercrime
confidential informants (CIs), 64–65

corporate theft, 77–78
crack users, 36
credit cards
    cloning, 51, 53, 55
    as incoming mail target, 35–36
    monitoring statements, 9, 53
    skimming, 48–52
    suspicious transactions, 53–54
credit ratings, 11
cybercrime
    catching thieves, 76–80
    definition of, 70
    hijacking computers for, 80
    investigating, 76–80
    preventing, 86–91

D
Department of Homeland Security, 67
Department of Motor Vehicles (DMV), 66
digital footprints, 77
Disneyland Park, 62
documents
    forensic laboratories and, 66–67, 69
    used by terrorists, 62, 66–67
driver's licenses, 18–20, 24, 57–58, 62, 66
drug addicts, 34, 36

E
E.H. Ferree wallet makers, 42
e-mail, 75, 78, 80–84
EMV microchip transactions, 56
encoders, 52
evidence
    cybercrime and, 76–80, 86
    fingerprints as, 28–30

F
Facebook, 74, 89
fake ATM, 50–51
fake ID, 22, 24, 32, 90
FBI (Federal Bureau of Investigation), 8, 14–15, 70, 77, 85
federal agencies
    FBI, 8, 14–15, 70, 77, 85
    GAO, 65–66
    ICE, 65–68
    USPS (semi-independent), 39, 43
Federal Reserve, 27
Federal Trade Commission, 9, 25, 27
felony, 43
fingerprints, 28–30
Forbes, 74
foreign countries, 87
forensics analysts, 78–79, 83
forensic laboratories, 66–67, 69

G

garbage sifting, 36–37
Google, 91
Government Accountability Office (GAO), 65–66
GPS, 25
greed, 28, 53, 75

H

heroin addicts, 36
Hmimssa, Youssef, 62, 64
hotel room keys, rewriting, 55

I

identity theft, definition of, 6–7
identity theft rings, 12, 34, 39, 86–87
Immigration and Customs Enforcement (ICE), 65–68
impersonation, 57, 81, 85, 90
inks, 22, 64, 67–68
Instagram, 89–90
Integrated Automated Fingerprint Identification System (IAFIS), 30
Internet
 black markets on, 84
 forgeries and, 57–58
 phishing on, 81–83
 sale of identification on, 72
 sale of passports on, 68–69
 See also cybercrime
Internet protocol (IP) address, 80, 83, 86

K

Kincaid, Steve, 21

L

laboratories, forensic, 66–67, 69
latent prints, 28–30
law enforcement
 catching thieves, 15, 25, 37, 70, 78
 CIs and, 64–65
 drug addicts and, 34
 forensic experts and, 76–77
 future of, 86–87
 greed of thieves aiding, 28, 53, 75
 interrogations and, 40–41
 investigations, 14–15
 passports and, 67
 profiling software and, 54
 Social Security number importance and, 61
 on technology, 31
 thieves caught, 21, 25
 See also federal agencies
Lebanese Loop, 48

Los Angeles, CA, 36, 39

M
mail-boxers, 34, 37, 39
Massey, Stephen, 36
meth addiction, 34–36
microprinting, 68
Minnesota, 12, 22, 25, 40, 84
misspellings, 26, 50
Morris, Mike, 77

N
Nigerian Prince scam, 82
New York City, 80
New York Times, 62
ninhydrin, 29–30
North Carolina, 61

O
online banking, 89
Operation Firewall, 85

P
passports
  as breeder document, 58
  color-shifting inks on, 68
  ease of forging, 57–58, 68
  fingerprints and, 30
  microprinting on, 68
  sale of, 68–69
  terrorists and, 62, 67
personal checks, 23
Peterson, Brendan, 6
Peterson, David, 29
phishing, 81–83
PINs (personal identification numbers), 45–46, 48, 51
police. See law enforcement
police interviews, 40–41, 76, 78
prison, 21, 43
profiling software, 54
public computers, 89

R
Rawson, Richard, 35–36
remote hacking, 80

S
Secure Hash Algorithm 1 (SHA-1), 91
sexual harassment, 84
shoulder-surfing, 23, 46–47
silver nitrate, 29
skimmers, 48–52
Snapchat, 89
social media, 25, 89–90
Social Security numbers
  Abraham Abdallah and, 74–75

black market and, 84
as breeder document, 58
corporate theft and, 72, 74
ease of forging, 57–58
first identity theft and, 42
importance of, 61–62
on incoming mail, 34
phishing and, 81–82
remote hacking and, 80
undocumented immigrants and, 58–59, 61, 65
Spielberg, Steven, 75

T
Target stores, 73
terrorists, 62, 67

U
undocumented immigrants, 58–59, 61, 65
U.S. Congress, 65–66
U.S. Postal Service (USPS), 39, 43

V
victims
annual number of, 8, 10
consequences for, 10–12
probable first, 42
thieves caught by, 37
thieves known to, 21–22
video cameras, 25, 37, 53, 55
Virginia, 61

W
washing checks, 22–23, 28
Whitcher, Hilda, 42
Winfrey, Oprah, 75
Wisconsin, 12, 44

Photo Credits

Cover supernitram/iStock/Thinkstock; p. 7 ESB Professional/Shutterstock.com; pp. 8, 13 New York Daily News Archive/Contributor/New York Daily News/Getty Images; p. 11 Andrey_Popov/Shutterstock.com; p. 14 AP Photo/Nick Ut; p. 17 Cheryl Savan/Shutterstock.com; p. 19 Georgejmclittle/Shutterstock.com; p. 20 Bob Jacobson/Corbis/Getty Images; p. 24 Janaka Dharmasena/Hemera/Thinkstock; p. 26 Jim Wilkes/Contributor/Toronto Star/Getty Images; p. 29 PAUL J. RICHARDS/Staff/AFP/Getty Images; p. 33 Alexey Stiop/Shutterstock.com; p. 35 Fotosenmeer/Shutterstock.com; p. 38 Ken Wolter/Shutterstock.com; p. 41 Mediaphotos/Shutterstock.com; p. 42 Charlotte Observer/Contributor/Tribune News Service/Getty Images; p. 45 Gang Liu/Shutterstock.com; p. 47 Image Source/Image Source/Getty Images; p. 49 pspn/Shutterstock.com; p. 51 Danny Lawson/PA Wire; p. 59 rSnapshotPhotos/Shutterstock.com; p. 60 LilliDay/E+/Getty Images; p. 63 STEPHAN AGOSTINI/Stringer/AFP/Getty Images; p. 65 Scott Olson/Staff/Getty Images News/Getty Images; p. 67 Justin Sullivan/Stringer/Getty Images News/Getty Images; p. 71 Yurich84/iStock/Thinkstock; p. 73 AP Photo/Steven Senne, File; p. 79 Bloomberg/contributor/Bloomberg/Getty Images; p. 81 Jerry Cleveland/Contributor/Denver Post/Getty Images; p. 85 AP Photo/Jacquelyn Martin.

About the Author

Sarah Machajewski is a professional writer who holds a dual degree in English literature and history from the University of Pittsburgh. She is the author of more than 200 books for children and young adults. A true lover of words and explorer of ideas, Machajewski currently lives in Buffalo, N.Y., surrounded by books and their infinite possibilities.